Successful Strokes

A Realistic Guide to Creating a
Lucrative Massage Business

Praise for *Successful Strokes - A Realistic Guide for Creating a Lucrative Massage Business*

Bestseller on Amazon in Massage and Health Books

"Molly Kurland, massage professional, has shared her knowledge and wisdom in her new book, *Successful Strokes: A Realistic Guide to Creating a Lucrative Massage Business*. The book takes us through the process of navigating the trials and tribulations of starting your own massage business. Covering everything from basics in marketing to accounting, to avoiding burnout, this book is well thought out, helpful, and probably a good bet for anyone looking to start their own business. The addition of links and websites that you can use for additional tools in your own progress and success was very nice. I particularly enjoyed the friendly and approachable tone that Molly takes in her writing. You really feel like she cares about you and making your business successful. Her knowledge and accessibility make her a great author, particularly for the self-help variety of books. Successful Strokes offers insightful tips and tricks that a seasoned veteran of the massage business has learned along her own journey. Molly supplies materials, lists, and appointment schedule examples to help even the most novice massage therapist get started. Many of the tips were also helpful to an entrepreneur not involved with massage, just business. Overall, a great read for any business-minded masseuse!"

Reviewed by Katelyn Hensel for Readers' Favorite

"This book has helped me. I am terrible with the admin and marketing but love and am good at giving the massages. Thank you."

Nicole Armstrong, MA, Successful Strokes Facebook Page

"Molly, I love your book, and your guided meditation—of which I am a HUGE fan, in general—has been very helpful. Thanks SO much. I'm determined (yet very scared!) to make a comfortable living doing massage therapy. Your knowledge is helpful, as well as reassuring. Glad I found you here on Facebook."

G. Levine, Massage Therapist, E. Longmeadow, MA, Successful Strokes Facebook Page

"Practical, engagingly friendly, full of savvy advice, & grounded in the reflection of experience. I enjoyed Molly's honesty and empathy for others, in sharing her endeavors in opening and running a successful professional massage practice. I'm a massage therapist with 20 years' experience & I gathered some interesting new ideas!"

Wendy Levy, Massage Therapist, Windsor, CA, Amazon Review

"Molly I just finished reading your book. It is amazing! Thank you! It has given me a lot of inspiration. I have been a massage therapist for 5 years and I needed some direction. Your book has given that to me."

Janet Thompson, Dayton, OH, Successful Strokes Facebook Page

"A very thorough and detailed book that can assist any holistic healthcare practitioner in their private practice. Thank you, Ms. Kurland, for sharing your experience and expertise. Starting up your own practice? Get this book!"

J. Callahan, Volcano, HI, Amazon Review

I will not die an unlived life.

I will not live in fear

of falling or catching fire.

I choose to inhabit my days,

to allow my living to open me,

to make me less afraid,

more accessible,

to loosen my heart

until it becomes a wing,

a torch, a promise.

I choose to risk my significance;

to live so that which came to me as seed

goes to the next as blossom

and that which came to me as blossom,

goes on as fruit.

fully alive - dawna markova

Successful Strokes

A Realistic Guide to Creating a
Lucrative Massage Business

Molly Kurland

Dedicated to all the brave souls
who have taken risks to follow their dreams.

Table of Contents

INTRODUCTION: BALANCING IDEALISM AND PRACTICALITY

This is the story of how a quiet, introspective person created a successful massage practice. I may not enjoy giving presentations in front of large groups, but I am good at figuring out what people want. If you give people what they want, they will come back. I learned that, for the most part, they did not want to come to my home. They wanted set hours. They wanted the phone answered. They often wanted to get a massage the same day they called, sometimes right away. They wanted focused, personal attention, and they wanted my service to be convenient and easy for them to use.

I will share with you all the knowledge I have gained from decades in the field of massage, and from the journey of creating my own business. Given the nature of your own personality and style, there may be certain things you choose to do differently. As long as you follow legal guidelines, there is no right or wrong way to run a business. Just do what works.

There are as many styles of business as there are types of people. Many things were suggested to me over the years that just did not suit my personality, so I didn't do them. For example, people often suggested groups they could arrange to have me speak to, but I didn't feel comfortable addressing a room full of people. I thanked them for the opportunity but I declined. I found other ways to promote myself and I succeeded anyway. And so will you.

I will show you how to choose a good location, set up a professional office, hang out your shingle and get started as a massage therapist in private practice. By paying close attention to the details as you set it all up, you will have a business you'll be proud to invite anyone to, including other health professionals. As you follow the principles I outline of how best to nurture your clientele, you will develop a loyal following. This will enable you to live well, take vacations, and buy the things you want—all with the income from your massage practice.

I'll teach you how to set up business records, market yourself, and build up your clientele. In addition to this basic business information, I will also address some of the more personal issues of having a private practice. You will see how to manage relationships with your clients, set your own boundaries and take care of yourself so you don't experience burnout.

Through the anecdotes I share about my own journey, you will find that it's okay to be experimental and make a few mistakes along the way while still becoming a success. I certainly did, and there was no one to show me the way. With any new endeavor, there's always a certain amount of trial and error. Every successful person will tell you they tried things that didn't work. But they shrugged it off and tried something else until they figured it out. That's what you will do. As long as you learn the lessons from what happens and make changes accordingly, you'll be fine. And hey, some of those blunders that seemed so daunting at the time will turn into funny stories when you are rehashing it all with your friends.

How I Got Started

My introduction to massage began in the late '70s when a friend of mine had just completed a massage course and offered to practice on me. That massage was one of the most profound experiences I'd ever had. I'm quick with my mind, and am good at rationalizing and analyzing, but the bodywork cut through all that. You can't fool the body. The body doesn't lie. At the time that my friend was practicing on me, I was going through the breakup of my first serious relationship. My body was full of emotions, many of them confusing and contradictory. I was in college, majoring in psychology. I was well aware of the cognitive reasons for what I was going through. But understanding things intellectually was not helping. I still felt miserable and emotionally overwhelmed. The massages I received from my friend really helped me progress and to rid myself from years of stress and tension I had been carrying. I was fortunate to be receiving a massage every week. As the weeks passed, I became lighter, freer, and happier. I could feel my personality changing from being a shy, quiet person, to one who spoke up and took risks. I was awestruck by the powerful impact massage was having on my life.

I was very interested in studying massage and thought that perhaps I could combine traditional counseling with bodywork in order to use a more holistic approach to psychotherapy. I wasn't sure how it all would fit together, but continued with a strong sense of the importance of what I was learning. The only thing I was absolutely certain of was that this would improve my life.

So I dove into the friendly world of strokes, hugs, and massage therapy. I found a small massage school that I had heard about from a fellow student, called The Sonoma School of Wholistic Massage. It was a fairly new school and didn't have premises yet, so our classes were held in the instructor's home. There were only eight students, creating a very relaxed, intimate atmosphere. The twice-weekly massage class gave me an opportunity to be nurtured and touched at the same time I was learning a skill.

What I Learned About a Home-Based Practice

I never did become a licensed counselor. I began giving massages to friends and neighbors while I was completing my education. I didn't charge a lot, but it was a fairly lucrative and pleasurable way to earn money. For the next five years I gave massages, working from my home and occasionally in health clubs. I loved introducing people to the deep relaxation of therapeutic massage.

There were, however, many drawbacks to giving massages at home. First of all, I always felt on call. If the phone rang, I answered it, whether it was daytime, nighttime, or the weekend, whether I'd just come out of the shower or was in the middle of preparing dinner. If the phone rang, it might be a paying client. I became a slave to the phone. It was also very hard to set work hours and non-work hours. If someone wanted a massage, I did whatever I could to rearrange my life to fit them in. Does this sound familiar?

Another problem was the lack of professionalism that resulted from working at home. I do know many people who practice at home in a very professional manner. They have a special massage room set up, with a tidy waiting area, and they manage to do their business in a relaxed, yet professional environment.

But I didn't do any of this. I set up my massage table in the living room, had no furniture except for some large pillows on the floor and a mattress covered with a colorful bedspread that served as a couch.

I made a few other innocent mistakes. I had one phone number that I used for everything. I ran an ad in one of those free ad newspapers that people generally use for selling cars and appliances. And I quite unconsciously wore a cotton tank top and drawstring pants, which were very comfortable for doing massage work.

I couldn't understand why so many male clients seemed to want some kind of additional service from me. After all, I gave very good therapeutic massages. I kept my clients covered with a sheet, and I thought I was behaving professionally. But one week I had a series of male clients and they all wanted some kind of sexual addition. I was quite nervous and embarrassed! I spilled out my confusion with a friend, who replied, "This wouldn't have anything to do with the fact that you are giving these men massages while dressed suggestively in a room with a mattress on the floor, would it?"

Boundaries were another issue that became complicated by working at home. People frequently arrived late for their appointments and wanted to hang around and visit long after their massages were finished. Because I wasn't in a business environment, people didn't take me as seriously as I would have liked. They often behaved as though massage was something I did for fun between baking bread and pruning the roses. I needed to work to create an atmosphere of professionalism when working at home. One home-based massage therapist I knew, greeted her clients at the door wearing a white lab coat. It gave them a quick, visual message!

I continued to practice massage in my home while I finished my undergraduate work. This massage practice was the first time I really loved doing something that was also bringing me money. I had many experiences where I enjoyed working with clients so much I felt almost guilty that I was getting paid. The reward of how good I was able to make them feel made my life feel worthwhile and full of higher purpose.

Planning the Next Step

After I graduated college, I got married and my husband and I took an extended trip around the world. For nearly two years, we traveled to the South Pacific, Australia, Southeast Asia, and Great Britain. This trip was an opportunity to have some time to reflect on my life and what I wanted, before I settled into the world of responsibilities. It was probably the last time I would ever be this free.

My long, slow journey gave me a great deal of time to think about what I wanted to do when I returned to the United States. I was convinced that massage was my path. I made friends everywhere by giving locals massages, relieving headaches, and neck and shoulder pain. I quickly became popular wherever I happened to be. Every interaction confirmed my desire to set myself up in a massage career.

I thought about the best way to set up a massage practice when I returned. I still wanted to live in Sonoma County, California. I had close friends there and I loved the beauty of the area. It has always felt like home. I began thinking about the kind of place I would ideally like to have. I wanted to create a soothing environment that would appeal to all types of clients, as well as being a great atmosphere in which to work.

When I returned, I was surprised that no one else had created the kind of massage practice that I had been dreaming of. But back then, that was not the way massage was practiced. People either worked at a health club, a chiropractic office, a resort in Calistoga, or out of their homes. I was the only person at that time to open a massage office that was set up in the style of a health professional.

By the time I returned home to Sonoma County from my long trip abroad, I had thought through so many details of my first massage office that I had it open within a couple of months of settling back in. I had a pretty good idea of how I wanted it to look, and what I wanted it to contain. I had bought some beautiful batik fabric while in Indonesia, so I used that as a decorative touch to give it some colorful accents.

I had a room with a hot tub and shower, a massage room, and a tiny waiting room. After a couple of years, I shared the office with another therapist who came in a couple of days a week when I wasn't working.

The general public was not in the habit of getting massages the way people do today. I got some people who were indulging themselves in a rare treat. Others came in because they had a muscular pain that wasn't being treated adequately by traditional medicine. This inspired me to learn more pain relief techniques and opened my eyes to the role massage could play in the mix of health care.

I will be discussing the importance of presenting yourself in a professional manner throughout this book. There are many subtleties that can make the difference between whether people want to be your client for a long time or whether they don't come back. Surprisingly, many excellent massage therapists are unaware of how their environment and their behavior can make such a huge difference to clients.

When I first started, there were no books on how to start a massage business. In fact, business was not even taught as part of the curriculum in massage schools. It was totally up to me to present massage to my community in a way that would be respected so I could build a reliable clientele. This was a puzzle I decided I wanted to solve.

Having my own massage practice was my dream, and I wanted to see my vision become a reality. I honestly could not imagine doing anything else. I believed deeply in the benefits of massage and I was convinced that if presented in the right way, a massage practice could thrive. Thus, I put myself in my customer's shoes. I tried various approaches. I learned what worked and what didn't work. When something didn't work, which happened much of the time, I tried something else. I made many mistakes. I learned a lot on my way to becoming successful. My gift to you is sparing you the many years of financial and emotional expense it took to get me there.

CHAPTER 1: YOUR PRESENTATION SPEAKS VOLUMES

What makes a massage practice successful? The secret to having your appointment book as full as you want it all year round involves giving your clients an exceptional experience. There are many little details about the way you present yourself and your business that can make a big difference in the way people perceive you. I will keep coming back to this theme as we discuss everything you do and how it affects your client. There are numerous reasons people keep coming back to a massage therapist, and only one of them has to do with receiving a wonderful massage. There are things you can do to make your client's visit so restorative that they will look forward to their next session the moment they leave your office. In addition, they will want to share you with everyone they know!

What is Meant by "Presentation?"

Your presentation includes how you show the world who you are, what you do, and how you do it. People pick up on these cues and it affects the way they feel. It all makes a difference. The location of your office, as well as the way it is decorated and organized, will make coming to see you more or less attractive, depending on how quiet and appealing the environment is. Every single aspect of your client's experience matters. From the ease at which they are able to get an appointment, to the way the room looks and smells, the way you are dressed, how much you talk, what you talk about—every moment has an effect on your client. They are coming to see you because they want to feel better. They are either stressed or in pain—or both—and they are looking for relief. Since massage deals so much with the senses, it is necessary to consider how your environment affects them.

Some Things to Consider:

- Location of your office
- Signage
- Your appearance
- How you greet your clients
- How you engage before and after the session
- Lighting
- Music
- Scents

- Street sounds
- Sounds of other office tenants

The way you present yourself shows your client how much thought you have put into your practice. That will translate into how well you intend to take care of them.

Think of the analogy of going out to eat. Imagine a fine restaurant, in a beautiful location, perhaps with an outdoor patio surrounded by a garden. The waiter comes to take your order and elaborately describes the food, making sure you're getting exactly what you want. Your food is brought to you on a beautiful plate that is artfully arranged with decorative edible garnishes. You can see that all of the ingredients are of the highest quality. Care was taken to make it interesting and creative as well as delicious. Now, contrast that with the same basic food, but now in a crowded, noisy eatery. Imagine the food with similar ingredients, put on the plate in no particular arrangement, placed in front of you on a plastic laminate table with artificial flowers. The server is busily squeezing you in among all the other people they have to serve. It's practically the same food. But it's a very different presentation in a very different environment.

If you're simply hungry and want a quick, cheap meal the latter will suffice. But if what you want is a truly nurturing experience of recharging your energy and spirit as well as your tummy, you're going to want to go to the first place. You'll be willing to pay more for that experience because you're getting much more than a meal. You're also receiving a deeply needed break.

That is what your client is looking for, too. They are seeking out a deeply needed break, as well.

Be Authentic

One of the secrets to success is being true to yourself. It's important to create a business environment that truly resonates with you. After all, your personality and style will attract your clients just as much as your method of bodywork. Thus, you want to do things in a way that really excites you, paying close attention to every aspect of your business. When you are thrilled about what you're doing, your enthusiasm is infectious. That's what clients respond to—that gorgeous light that shines in your eyes when you are in a place that really makes you happy. They see that glow and it lights them up, too!

From your new client's first contact with you, they are developing a feeling about you and about your practice. They are often stressed and in pain, and they are coming to you in order to feel better. Therefore, everything you can do to make their experience easy and pleasant makes a difference. As we go deeper into the specifics of creating your practice, I want you to think about things that either attract you or turn you off to different people with whom you have done business. What makes you want to go back, and what or makes you hesitate?

As you reflect on this, people may come to mind who do excellent work in their field, but who present themselves in a way that is uncomfortable or unpleasant.

Showing Up Like a Professional

Taking your work from your home into a costly office is a big leap, yet I believe it to be an essential step. Many people I have spoken with cannot understand what difference it makes to a client. However, one experience I had validated the importance of having a professional environment.

I had a client, an insurance agent, who mentioned to me that she was interested in trying acupuncture to get some relief from headaches. She asked if I had ever tried it or knew anything about it. I had a friend who was an acupuncturist who I liked very much, and I referred my client to her. Susan practiced acupuncture in her home.

When Lynda returned for her next massage I asked her how the acupuncture went. She told me it had been a terrible experience. Now remember, this woman had never experienced acupuncture before. So she had all the trepidation about someone sticking needles in her as well as a lack of familiarity with how oriental medicine works. She went to Susan's house, which is a nice enough place, and was shown into her acupuncture room—a converted bedroom with a massage table for her patients lie on. My client said that Susan inserted the needles, and then left the room. After a few minutes, Lynda heard Susan go into the kitchen and start washing her dishes!

Now, if you've ever had acupuncture, you know that there is a period of time after the needles are inserted when you are left alone for fifteen or twenty minutes to lie still. But you expect to have a quiet, peaceful environment, perhaps with some soft music playing. You do not expect the acupuncturist to go wash her dishes.

My client said that Susan's roommate came home and started playing his guitar, which was also very inappropriate. This unprofessionalism caused her to lose confidence in Susan, and turned her off to the whole experience of acupuncture. It didn't matter that Susan used the correct acupuncture points and could have helped Lynda's chronic headache pain. Lynda wasn't going to give her a chance.

Of course this referral made me look bad, because I was the one who recommended this terrible experience to her. Until this happened, I didn't understand how much difference an office environment could make. But I was able to see through my client's eyes, how Susan's personal life bled through into her acupuncture practice and made some people very uncomfortable.

You will be surprised how many people do not pay attention to their presentation. It amazes me how much this happens in the world of massage. This is a field that has so much to do with soothing the senses. Yet, I have been to therapists who work in places that are noisy, messy, smell bad from rancid massage oil and are cluttered with scraps of paper and personal belongings. I have had massages from people who don't stop talking, share way too much about their personal problems or spend the whole time giving me advice. It is always shocking to me that massage therapists can be so unaware of these things. Clients are usually too polite to give them negative feedback. Instead, they just don't come back— and then everybody loses. That's why paying attention to all the details will make a world of difference.

One of my favorite massage therapists has a downtown office on a quiet street. Her building is a converted apartment house with charming 1940s architecture shared with other professionals and therapists. Her suite consists of a waiting room containing a couple of upholstered chairs and beautiful decorative furnishings in an art deco style. The massage room has a small fountain that bubbles softly in the background amid low light and soft music. It is obvious that all the furniture and art have been carefully chosen with relaxation in mind. After the massage, she offers homemade, healthy snacks and a choice of hot or iced tea. She schedules 30 minutes between each client so there is time to rest and recoup before returning to the world. She totally understands the concept of presentation.

Taking the Plunge

The main reason massage practitioners want to practice at home is to keep costs down. And it does make a difference not to have several hundred dollars of office rent to worry about each month. But I'll tell you, once you rent that office, you really make a commitment to your business. It changes things. Not only do your clients take you more seriously, *you* take yourself more seriously. As long as you are working at home and have minimal overhead, you don't have to care as much. If you don't want to work, you don't. If you decide to take off for a vacation, you take off. If a party comes up on a day you usually work, you just don't schedule any clients that day. The point I'm making is this—until you make a serious commitment to your practice, there is a sense that if things don't work out, that's okay. You haven't invested much.

Many people practice massage in this manner. Probably the majority of people who go through massage school end up doing a little bit of massage at home on the side. There's nothing wrong with that. Massage is a wonderful experience. However it is practiced, massage helps make the world a better place. Whether you give a few massages a week to some friends, chair massages in an airport, or a full aromatherapy treatment in a spa, you are giving out relaxing, healing energy. You are helping to soften someone's hard edges. You are making people lighter, softer, and more sensitive, and they will carry those feelings with them to the next person they encounter. Doing massage in any capacity creates a positive ripple effect.

Creating a Safe Space

In my business, I gave many people their first massages. It was very important that I create a safe space for them to relax. Over and over again, they told me what a nice place I had and that they had always wanted a massage but didn't know where to go. It is not as difficult today as it was twenty years ago to find a nice place to get a massage, but the principle is the same. Massage clients are going to take off their clothes and let a stranger touch them. They want to do this in a place that they feel is non-threatening and appropriate. That is why it is so important to go out of your way to create an atmosphere of professionalism, where they can feel secure.

Your home is not a safe, neutral space, which is what many people need in order to feel comfortable. In your home, people can smell what you cooked for breakfast. They can hear your neighbor's kids. While there is nothing wrong with your personal life, this is not what your clients want to see. They want you to be in the role of healer and caretaker for them. They do not necessarily want to know that much about your life and your problems. Later on I will go into more detail about the grey areas between professional and personal relationships and how they sometimes overlap. Right now we are discussing establishing yourself as a professional in an environment that supports you.

The space in which you practice massage affects you, too. You are much more easily distracted in your home than you would be in an office. Someone comes to the door. You get a text message. You forgot to take something out of the freezer for dinner. There are stacks of mail you've been meaning to open. There are so many distractions at home that it is much harder for you to be present and focus completely on your client and they can sense this. It's easy for clients to feel that they are interrupting you when they come to your home, because often you were absorbed in some personal activity just before they arrived. This is one more reason it is harder to build a clientele working out of your home than in an office.

You may argue that there are some people who would mind a home office and some who wouldn't, and you are only interested in working with those who don't mind. We will get into this later when we talk about marketing and identifying your target market. I think by now you realize that whereas anyone would feel comfortable in an office, only certain people would feel fine coming to your home. Wouldn't it serve you best in the long run to have an environment where you could feel proud to invite anyone?

Over the next few chapters, I will elaborate about the best way to set up your office, organize your professional life, manage your finances, develop successful marketing techniques, and have fun during the process. Let's go!

The Essence of Chapter One:

- Your presentation includes all the details that affect your client's experience.
- Your environment needs to be neat, organized, and neutral.
- The sounds must be quiet and soothing.
- The lighting should be dim.
- Odors and aromas must be pleasing.
- Your behavior should be professional and focused on your client in order to put them at ease.

CHAPTER 2: CREATING YOUR IMAGE

Whether you realize it or not, you are projecting messages about yourself and your business all the time. Whether you are purposely crafting a certain type of image, or you are just winging it, you are making an impression on the public that affects how they see you.

The Difference Between Presentation and Image

Your image conveys what you do—the type of bodywork that is your specialty. Your presentation is how you express that to your client and it includes the look, feel, and sounds of both your environment and the way you behave. The way you present your image helps your client understand how you're going to help them. It lets them know whether your focus is on stress reduction, pain relief, sports injuries, medical massage, aromatherapy, or a combination of those. It's important to communicate this, both with your words and what you show them, so they can feel at ease with you and have appropriate expectations.

When I started practicing massage in 1976, the word "massage" was most widely used as a cover-up for prostitution. The type of holistic massage I had learned was considered a new, alternative health practice, which has become incorporated into mainstream culture over the years. And I say, thank goodness to that!

Even so, the fact that massage was so misunderstood when I began to practice helped drum it into me how important it was to define the image I wanted to project, and to present it well. I live in one of the most forward thinking, trendsetting parts of the country, and I still meet many people who have never had a massage and are both curious and nervous about it.

Choosing Your Niche

Think about the type of person you are and the kind of practice you want to have. Is there a theme to the style of practice you want to create?

Do you participate in sports? Do you want to focus on athletes? This can work as a niche. If you ride horses, you may want to promote yourself to the equestrian set. Allow your practice to have a flavor that is an extension of who you are.

Maybe your dream is to create the most soothing and relaxing environment possible as an escape from our hectic world. Thus you'd be incorporating calming colors and textures in your decor with framed pictures of plants and flowers on the walls, and strategically placed vases full of fresh flowers. You might include aromatherapy and herbs into your practice.

If you want to focus on medical massage, such as working on injuries and people who've been in accidents, you may want to create a more clinical setting. In your office you might have lots of educational literature on subjects such as how to properly lift, exercises to strengthen various muscles, and the benefits of regular exercise. You can have muscle, nerve and skeletal charts on the walls so you can show clients their anatomy and help them understand what they may have done to injure themselves.

My focus was on relaxation, even though people did come to me for help with other things, such as headaches and muscle pain. But mainly I wanted to help relieve stress. In fact, I even studied hypnosis so I could help people relax their busy minds. The combination of hypnosis and massage allowed my clients to let go so they could receive the deep nurturing they needed. The environment I created was very soothing. I used pastel colors and a lot of soft fabrics to decorate my office, so that the moment my client walked through the door they were in another world, and one that they associated with leaving their concerns behind.

If you want to have a varied practice, focus on creating a basic professional, high-quality persona. Keep your space clean and uncluttered. Have one or two pieces of nice furniture and a beautifully framed photograph or painting. That's all you need to set the stage for a great work space.

The Sexual Perception of Massage

Although things have improved a great deal since I began practicing massage, there are still many people who carry the old notion that massage is really an open door to all manner of sexual gratification. Indeed, there are still establishments in almost every town that thrive on offering genital massages. It is understandable, then, that some people have this apprehension.

In the beginning of this book, I described how I naively set up business in my living room, wearing a tank top and no bra, with a mattress on the floor that served as my "couch." Of course, I did not consciously think about creating an image at that time, but I certainly was creating one—and it was not at all the image I wanted to create!

There are two things I want to address here. The first is that you have to be careful that your office does not present you in a suggestive manner. For instance, the mattress on the floor in my living room could have been construed as the next step after the massage table. You don't want anything your client sees to be the basis of a misunderstanding. Since many forms of massage can be quite sensual, if that is the flavor of your practice you have to be very clear and careful where and how you draw the line. Candles and low lighting are soothing and acceptable, but you need to take care that the massage room looks like a treatment room and not your boudoir.

The second is that the manner in which you behave, as well as the way you dress, will be essential to giving your client the proper message. If your massage and your atmosphere tend toward the sensual, your clothing should be more tailored and businesslike to convey to your client that you are a therapist. You will also need to use a more formal manner in speaking to your clients, explaining to them a little bit about the session, what they are expected to do, and what they can expect of you. Do not act mysterious, shy, quiet, or submissive in any way. If you are a woman meeting male clients, you especially need to take charge of the situation and project an aura of confidence, expertise, and control. If you do not have these feelings inside, you need to do whatever inner work will allow you to feel that way. Your client is looking to you to set the stage.

Women must remember that men have sex on their minds a lot. Although they usually do not act on their thoughts, they are always looking for signals from a woman to let them know whether she is open to sexual behavior. In a massage situation, where this can be ambiguous, it is your job to make things very clear. Clients will respond to whatever message you give them, verbally as well as non-verbally.

Male therapists need to be aware that women may be a little nervous about being touched by a man they don't know, even though they do want to receive a massage. You must take care to put them at ease, giving them the necessary privacy so that they can disrobe and get ready without feeling exposed. Again, giving out that the air of confidence and professionalism will help them relax and feel safe with you.

Working Through Your Own Issues

During the period when I was doing massage in my living room, I became very anxious about the sexual tension I perceived during many of the sessions. I could sense that the men wanted something from me, although no one actually asked for anything sexual. The tension became so thick that one week it was almost all I could think of. It had to do with the way men stared at me while I worked on them. I felt it in the way they brushed against me, or the way they subtly tried to touch me back, especially when I was massaging their hands. Sometimes it seemed as though any second I was going to be grabbed.

One week, every single man asked if there was any more to the massage than what he was already getting. Even clients who had been coming to me for several months suddenly asked if there was something else. When I went to see my therapist that week, I told her about this. "Well, of course," she said, "it's all you're thinking about! You expect every man to ask for something, and so he does!"

To put it bluntly, I was not in control of the situation. I was not comfortable about my sexuality, and I was not comfortable with their sexuality. I was not able to talk about sex or to ask them what was going on for fear that they would tell me. If I was going to go any farther in my career, I had some psychological work to do.

I did my work.

Years later, when I was in my office one evening, a young man came in for a massage. As I worked on him, he kept opening his eyes and twisting his head around to look at me. By this time I knew what he was thinking by his behavior. I think I may have even raised my eyebrows to invite a question.

"You don't %#@$*!?" he asked.

I laughed. He asked it in such a sweet, innocent way. By this time, I had no anxiety at all about this kind of thing because I had worked through it. I proceeded to give him a long lecture about the dangers of paying strangers for sex, discussed sexually transmitted diseases, and in the manner of an older sister, gave him some advice.

The man ended up thanking me for the massage, and said he would tell his aunt, who suffered from a bad back about me.

The Phone

You will inevitably get phone calls from people who are feeling you out as to whether or not your massage is sexual, regardless of your gender. In all the years of my practice, I have never had anyone come right out and ask me over the phone. You need to know what to listen for, and when you are sure they are asking for something you don't do, you must bring this up in the conversation. Otherwise you are inviting trouble, an embarrassing situation for both of you, and a waste of your time.

Here are some questions you might be asked to test the waters:

"What do you look like?"

"What are you wearing?"

"Do you massage the whole body?"

"Is this a sensual massage?"

"Is this a complete massage?"

"Do you do half and half?"

"Do you do extras?"

When I hear these obvious cues, my response is always,

"Are you looking for something sexual?"

Affirmative response.

"Well, you have called the wrong place. I only do therapeutic massage. Please find someone else." Click. Do not beat around the bush. If they deny it, find out what they meant by their question. It is unlikely that they will be asking the above questions and looking for a therapeutic massage.

There was, however, a man who called me one day and asked what I would be wearing during the massage session.

"Corduroy jeans and a white, short-sleeved shirt," I replied.

"Great!" the man responded. "The last place I went to, the woman was wearing a black negligee, and all I'm really looking for is a decent massage to work on my back pain." This gentleman became a regular bi-weekly client of mine for several years.

First Impressions Make a Big Difference

I once encouraged a friend in Michigan to get a massage. He told me that he had had massages while in the military, some of them sexual, some of them therapeutic. He finally went to get a massage, but he reported that the person did not do any real massage. She barely touched his muscles, and afterward asked if he would like any extras. He declined. I was horrified. How did he find her? He sheepishly admitted he'd seen a discount coupon in a direct-mail advertisement. He eventually found a good massage therapist whose prominent sign he passed on his way to work.

He described the experience to me in a letter:

"I want to tell you about the masseuse I visited last week. Yes, she is a member of that association you mentioned (American Massage Therapy Association) and she had several other official-looking plaques on the wall. Mind you, I'm not easily impressed by plaques! She works alone in an older brick building near the shopping center I live adjacent to. She shares the house with a beauty parlor, and has one room in which she works. The decor

in her room was sooo neat! I'll try to describe it some. I guess my overall impression was a New Age room with Victorian undercurrents, if that is imaginable. The wallpaper reminded me of the Roman Empire...it had large Roman numerals all over it and Latin words, but the characters were not bold, more like in shadow or watermark, but distinctly outlined. She had very heavy-duty wrought-iron curtain rods up, with a wire-framed ball on one end and a crescent moon on the other. These were above two windows. The curtains were a heavy, off-white lace type of thing and multi-layered with valances and all that stuff. She had a chest of drawers (I didn't look in them) and a chair that were antique oak and very nice; not too elaborate, not formal, but not country either. I don't remember a lot about the wall hangings but they were appropriate and not ostentatious. She had a brass shelf on one end and it was loaded with books on spiritual, philosophical, and mind-expanding subjects."

Notice how this client's eye tended to focus for a long time on the wallpaper and how the general decor and ambience seemed to set the stage for him. He was searching her style to get a sense of what to expect. It was a new experience for him. The attention to detail was not lost on him. It worked. It made a very positive impression. He continued seeing this massage therapist on a regular basis for a long time.

Other Image Considerations

Work Attire

In Chapter 1, I discussed the importance of setting up your office and having it uncluttered, with just a few pieces of good furniture. It is equally important to dress properly. After many years of practice, sixteen of which that were spent hiring other massage therapists, I have to say that some people naturally understand this and others need quite a bit of work. Most massage therapists I've known tend to be down-to-earth people who are not very concerned about what they wear, especially when they work. More often than not, their clothing will be casual, verging on ragged because they are more interested in being comfortable than stylish.

There is a balance between comfortable and professional clothing. You don't want to look as if you are struggling so hard that you can't afford to buy decent clothes. It will not inspire confidence in your clients to see you in T-shirts that are worn thin, or drawstring pants that are stretched from doing yoga. You don't want to look like you just finished doing yard work or washing your car either. Although this may sound obvious, I would not be bringing it up if I hadn't seen many massage therapists who dress inappropriately.

You want your clothes to be clean and fairly new, to fit properly, and to be stylish and professional. What does that mean? Professional attire does not include plunging necklines or mini skirts or oversized t-shirts. It does not include shorts or sweat pants. Nor does it necessitate a suit. You are, of course, going to be giving massages, possibly spilling oil on your clothes. And you need freedom of movement, so your clothes must be comfortable. There are many clothes available that are quite fashionable as well as easy to move in that will work well for you.

Coordinating Your Marketing with Your Image

In the early stages of developing your professional identity, you are designing the look and feel of your business. Your logo, specific colors, and any graphics that go with your business are things you will be incorporating when you start promoting yourself. Your visual image carries into everything that you do. Now is the time for you to be thinking about these things as you go through the process of defining your style of practice. In the chapter that deals with advertising, we will get into the specifics of what to do to market yourself.

I had a logo designed that was a line drawing of a woman's head with her eyes closed while a hand was in the process of an upward stroke on her neck. It was a quick, visual image that communicated relaxing massage.

Once you have decided on a category or niche for your business, have all your promotional materials coordinated with your image. When you have a logo designed, make sure it conveys the essence of your practice in a visual form. Your website, Facebook business page, business cards, and any literature or emails that you send out should all match. You're going to appear much more professional when everything you do is coordinated.

A graphic designer can help you with a lot of this. It is worth investing some money to set up this foundation because you will be using these basic tools that portray your image throughout your career.

When you brainstorm about how you will be advertising, look at what other, similar professionals are doing. You want to advertise in the same ways that high-quality, high-end (pricier), professional businesses do. This planning stage is critical to starting out right and saving you time and money in the long run. Make a list of things that you need to develop before you can begin marketing yourself.

- Your business name
- Your logo
- The font you use
- The colors you use
- Your style
- Any graphics in addition to your logo
- Business cards
- Brochures
- Website
- LinkedIn page
- Twitter account
- Facebook business page

A fun thing to do is to spend some time searching the web on massage therapists to get ideas. Right away, you will notice who is doing a good job of using graphic imagery to promote themselves and those who have taken a lot less care about the way they come across. What are you learning about each person by the way they promote their business image? Who appears to be someone who is probably good at what they do? On the internet, you only have a couple of seconds to get someone's attention. You want to make those seconds count.

Ready to get started and move into your office?

The Essence of Chapter Two

- Your image helps categorize the type of bodywork you do.
- Decide what your bodywork niche is.
- Through the use of your decor, your marketing materials, your signage, and the way you have set up your premises, your client will have an idea of what to expect from you.

CHAPTER 3:
SETTING UP YOUR OFFICE

What is the best place for you to set up your first massage office? How much should you pay for rent? Should your office be on the main drag or on a quiet street? What are important considerations?

These are some of the questions you should be asking yourself.

In this chapter I tell you what to look for in an office and how to set up your budget. Now we're getting to the fun part, where you can let your creative juices flow and start nailing things down.

There are many messages you send your clients with the premises you choose. Depending on the type of office you have, where it's located, and how it's decorated, your client will feel either welcome or intruding, relaxed or hectic, safe or vulnerable.

The location of your office and the environment you create will be pivotal to your practice. Your office must be easy to find, be conveniently located, have good parking, and have adequate space for everything you need to run your massage business. Setting up your office in a place that doesn't work for you can be a very costly mistake.

Organizing Your Budget

Before looking for a place to rent, you need to work out your budget. Your office must be affordable. So the next question is: how much space can you afford?

Here is my rule of thumb. The monthly rent for your office should be close to the cost of eight massage treatments. Thus, if you charge $75 per hour for massage, you can afford to spend $600/month on rent, more or less.

Since rent is only part of your expenses and you still have to pay for your phone, laundry, oils, advertising and office supplies I like to consider that one day of work per week covers your business overhead.

Let's say you see four clients per day.

$75 x 4 = $300 for one day's work

$300 x 4 weeks = $1200/month

Therefore, one day per week of seeing four clients brings you $1200 per month. Half of that, or $600, is your rent. The other half is for the rest of your business costs. Let's look at a typical monthly budget to get a sense of your total overhead:

Monthly Expenses:

Rent	$600
Laundry	$40
Telephone	$70
Advertising	$200
Oils, lotions and massage supplies	$50
Office supplies	$40
Total monthly expenses	**$1000**

If you're bringing in $1200 per month, per one day a week of work, and your monthly expenses are $1000, that gives you an additional $200 a month, or $2400 per year for one-time expenses, emergencies and incidentals. You will have yearly expenses, such as magazine subscriptions for your waiting room, annual association dues, insurance, and continuing education.

Of course, in reality, business fluctuates. One week may be busy with five clients a day, booked four days straight, and the next week may yield less business, or you may have cancellations. You need to work with a realistic average so you know how much money to allot for your office rent and things like advertising, which can eat up as many extra dollars as you care to spend.

When estimating a budget, it is important to err on the side of caution. Just in case you have a slow week, or an unexpected expense, you want to know that you have enough money. Always make a point of tucking some money in a savings account. It's important to build up savings so that you have money to fall back on in case you:

- Have a slow month
- Become ill and can't work
- Hear about a workshop you want to take
- Need a vacation
- Have to repair something that breaks

These financial considerations are in addition to your personal expenses. Some people use one checking and savings account both for their business and personal expenses. I don't recommend this. It is better to have both a separate checking and a separate savings account for each. This makes it much easier at tax time when you are calculating your deductible costs.

My Big Lesson

I rented my first office in 1981, and it cost me $185 per month. I was charging $30 per hour for massage back then, so I was paying a little less than the eight-massage rule suggests. It was a tiny office, and it was hidden in a complex amid other professional offices. When I first moved in, there were several other health care professionals - a chiropractor, an optometrist, a pediatrician, a podiatrist, a physical therapy office, a group of psychotherapists, and a speech therapist. It seemed like a good environment for my business, and the rent was reasonable.

The biggest drawback, however, was not its size. The real problem was that it was hidden. If you were driving by, you would not know a massage therapist was practicing there. Since all the offices were on the ground floor, surrounded by the parking lot, patrons of the other businesses did not even need to walk by my office to get to their destination. I got no advertising advantage from my location. I discovered this much, much later. The thing I loved about the office was the professional environment surrounded by other health practices and the price. The lesson I learned was: PAY FOR VISIBILITY.

This is another important factor when deciding how much rent to pay. How visible is a given location? Would you have signage? If you have an office on a main street with a big sign advertising massage and hundreds of people pass by there every day, that's a lot of advertising that you don't have to spend additional money for. Therefore, a prominent location would be worth the extra cost. I learned that I made more money by having a more expensive, visible location than having an inexpensive hidden one.

Many years later, I expanded my business into a day spa and moved it into a shopping center next to a large hotel and convention center. I had a big sign in front advertising our services. Everyone who approached the hotel or the shopping center saw our sign. Thousands of people noticed us on a regular basis. Many people dropped in to get information about our services or even to get an impromptu massage. That location was worth thousands of dollars in advertising. In fact, I only needed to do a minimal amount of additional advertising because so many people knew we were there.

Paying higher rent for a better location is another commitment to being in business. You are making more of an investment, but you are also setting yourself up for building your clientele more quickly and a more successful career. In the long run, I believe it's worth it.

Decor

There are several elements that need to be considered when setting up the interior of your office. It is important that your office appear soothing and relaxing to your client. It is just as important that you have everything you need there.

Focus on the Senses

The color you paint your walls should be among the cool colors that are soothing to look at. Plain white is fine. If you opt for colors, use cool colors in the blue, green, lavender spectrum. Keep it simple.

A few nice paintings can add to the ambience. Choose images from nature, or something relaxing, such as a mandala—nothing too bold a statement or too complex.

Be aware of sounds. Wind chimes outside the window, soft music, a small fountain can all help to minimize street sounds and help your client let go of the outer world while they are with you.

Aromatherapy with essential oils such as in a diffuser can add to the atmosphere, but many people are sensitive to scents. Citrus such as lemon, lemon verbena, bergamot, or woodsy scents such as cedar or rosemary are less problematic. Still, it's important to check in with your clients about this.

Keep Surfaces as Bare as Possible

Simple and uncluttered is the best strategy for your decor. Clutter contributes to stress and is a distraction for your clients and for you. Keeping accessories to a minimum will help your clients feel calm and relaxed.

Furniture should be minimal and comfortable. A small upholstered chair. A table here and there. A few pieces of artwork. A vase of flowers. A few artistic pieces. Not too much. There should be a few elements that are beautiful, that grab your client's attention for the few minutes they are looking around before they get ready for the massage, but that's all that's necessary. Have some attractive shelving units both with and without doors to store everything you need.

Keep your office as simple as possible so your clients don't become distracted by loose ends scattered here and there. You want to have everything you need easily at your disposal, with a minimum of furniture. Keep your business records and office materials out of the way under a roll top desk, behind cabinet doors, or otherwise hidden from public view.

Storage

There are a lot of supplies you will need room for, such as linens, massage supplies, books and business supplies so make sure there is room for some attractive storage furniture.

Shop around for cabinets, desks, filing cabinets so that you have places to keep everything you need and have it out of the way.

Your Creature Comforts

You will be living in this space. Create a beautiful work environment for yourself. Set up your shelves and storage furniture so that everything you need is easily accessible. One advantage of having the control over your life as a self-employed person is that you have the opportunity to make a wonderful place to spend your work day. What things do you need to enjoy your office? A comfortable chair to sit in between clients? A nice desk that is easy to organize?

There will also be personal things you will need room for. You'll be spending a lot of time in your office so there may be things you want to have for leisure time, such as books or

DVDs. You will probably want to have some dishes and a place to keep containers of tea, crackers, and non-perishable food items. YOU may even want to keep a small fridge, if there's room. I know one therapist whose office came with a small walk-in closet where she was able to have a mini fridge and set up a tiny kitchen.

Make sure there is room for everything you're going to want, both for your sessions with clients and for your own purposes when you are there in between sessions. Think about where everything will go so that they will be both accessible and out of sight.

My Setup

My office plan was to put in a hot tub for people to use before the massage. I found a small, rectangular, freestanding Jacuzzi hot tub that could be put into an office. I explained to my husband, who was going to do the carpentry and plumbing, that we were to divide this space into three tiny rooms: one for massage, one for the hot tub and shower, and one for a waiting room. He looked at this tiny space—about 280 square feet—and thought I was crazy.

I sat down with some graph paper and played with the little squares until I came up with a tight but workable plan. We carved three tiny rooms out of that space. The massage room itself was six feet by ten feet—just big enough for two feet of space all around the massage table. I don't recommend these dimensions. For eight years, I somehow managed to scuttle around in that tiny space. Because I am a small person, and I was able to maneuver in that mouse-sized massage room. I had some clients who were over six feet tall; their legs stuck off the end of the massage table, and they practically filled up the room. My largest client was 6'6" and weighed 300 pounds. Now when I think about that tiny room I don't know how I did it, but I was determined to make that place work for me.

The hot tub turned out to be a brilliant idea. There was no place like that. In fact, even today, other than a health club or spa, there are no private massage offices in town where I live that have a hot tub inside. It was not that hard to do and it made me stand out and extremely popular. My sessions included fifteen minutes of soak time before the treatment. People loved it.

Look carefully at the offices of people with whom you do business. Notice how the details of the environment make you feel—whether the place is spotlessly clean, whether there are piles of papers lying on the desk, and whether they have spent the effort to add decorative touches, or if they are sparse and purely functional. Notice if the environment and decor affects your confidence in their expertise. Pay attention to how you feel being in their workspace.

Start putting yourself in your client's shoes and imagine what kind of environment will be most appealing to them. Your business will only take off if you look at it from the point of view of your client.

Your Neighborhood

Will it matter to you to be located near interesting places to go for lunch, or walking distance from a park? Do you want to be near a good coffee shop? All of these considerations are part of the lifestyle you create while setting up your business.

It made a big difference for me to have some great places nearby to go when I had an hour or two between clients, where I could have a cup of tea, read the newspaper, meet someone for lunch, without having to go far. In fact, one of my favorite places to go was a Chinese restaurant three blocks away. I frequently showed up there at odd hours when I had a break, and since the restaurant wasn't too busy the owner would come and sit with me and talk. She eventually became a very good client of mine.

Another thing I enjoyed was being two blocks from a creek where I could take a walk on breaks during nice weather. It is fairly common that you will have an hour or two or three between clients and it can make a big difference in your quality of life if you have nice places to go nearby when you want to get out of the office during these times. Later on I will discuss uses of down time.

Transitioning from a Job to Your Own Office

Many people will take interim steps from working for someone else at a day spa, health club or resort to having their own place. There are compromises that can be made in order to make this change do-able. Realistically, to set up your own office from scratch you would have to have some capital, such as a loan or some funds to see you through the first couple of years while you are building up clientele on your way to having your business support you.

I got a loan that my mom co-signed. It not only gave me the capital to start my business, but it enabled me to build credit. It was also another thing that kept me committed. Whenever I would get frustrated or disappointed that things were not happening quickly enough (I can be very impatient!), knowing I had to pay that loan back kept me from giving up. It made me persevere and stick with it until I was financially self-sufficient.

Supplementing Your Massage Income

In addition to the loan, I also found some part-time work I could do that I was able to work around my client appointments. I am good at sewing and a friend connected me with a company that produced high-end kites that were made of beautiful applique designs. Every week, I picked up a bag of nylon pieces that were all cut out, and I sewed them onto the kites at home. It enabled me to work my own hours so I could be available for my clients while I still earned money to cover my bills. Between the loan and the part-time sewing job, I was able to become self-sufficient within a year. Depending on the economy and other factors, it could take longer. This is an endeavor which requires a certain amount of patience. It does take time to build up a steady clientele, but you will get there.

Many therapists use their offices part-time and are happy to rent them out to someone else the rest of the time. This is a very affordable way to start working for yourself while you still have another part-time job. You will still be in a professional environment, even if it's not completely your own. If it's someone else's office, you won't have total control over the way it is decorated and presented. But hopefully, this will just be for a year or two and then you will be able to find a place for yourself full-time.

You can also find office space to rent in salons, day spas, and healthcare offices. In many cases, these can also help introduce new clients to you.

Even if you start out part-time, you will be able to follow most of the suggestions in this book, even though this is written as though you are building it full-time from the beginning. If it is truly in your heart to have your own place and practice massage in your own unique style, there are many ways you can make that happen.

The Essence of Chapter Three

- Work out your budget so you know how much you can spend on office rent.
- Choose a visible location so it helps to advertise you, as well as be easy to find.

- Organize your space with sufficient cabinets and storage so that you have everything you need while your environment is simple and free of clutter.
- Make sure this location has the right feel and appropriate neighboring businesses so you and your clients will be comfortable with it.
- Find a neighborhood where you will enjoy spending your time, including down time so you will be happy there.

Chapter 4: Finances, Accounting, and Record Keeping

Setting up records and accounting systems was not the most fun part for me. I had a much better time putting up batik curtains and buying bouquets of flowers than organizing business records. But this is the heart of running a business. How you set up your records will determine whether things operate smoothly or get overwhelmingly out of control. It is important to set things up well to make administering your business simple. Once you get busy, you won't have time to go back and straighten out messes.

First of all, you need a good record keeping system where you can record money that comes in and money that goes out. This is important for when you do your taxes as well as a way to evaluate how you're doing financially.

I found it helpful to have a separate credit card for the business, even though it was in my personal name. That way I knew that every charge on my statement was tax-deductible.

I also kept an envelope for cash receipts—out-of-pocket expenses at the office supply store, small business purchases, business lunches, and so on. A dollar or two here and there can quickly add up to significant tax-deductible expenses.

Most massage businesses are conducted on a cash basis, meaning that people pay when they receive the service. There are a number of good accounting software programs. I liked Quicken made by the company, Intuit. I found it simple to set up and use. As part of your work, you may consider billing insurance companies. If so, you will need to keep track of your *accounts receivable* (money owed to you). This way you will know how much money is outstanding, and you'll be able to keep track of payments when they are received. Quickbooks, also by Intuit, is a bit more complex and has categories for this.

Pros and Cons of Insurance Billing

Automobile insurance companies and Worker's Compensation claims are often willing to pay for massages when an accident or injury occurs because if that can eliminate the individual's pain it is much cheaper to pay for a series of massages than to have to pay out a large settlement in a liability claim.

Advantages of Billing Liability Insurance Companies

When it works well, you have a contact at the insurance company to whom you send the bills and it only takes a few weeks to get paid. Make sure you get something in writing that authorizes the massage service. Find out who the agent is that is handling the case. Your client should have all this information. Often the approval is for a finite amount of treatments. Be certain that you have authorization for the sessions and that the company is prepared to "pay as you go," which means they will pay for each session and not wait for a case to be settled.

This can work very well for you and your client, in that they can get the treatment they need to recover from a whiplash or painful muscular injury. A client may come in once or twice a week for several months. If you are successful in helping them, the insurance company may even recommend you to other people in your area who have sustained injuries.

I did this for a while. I was able to help many people and it was incredibly rewarding work. It feels great to relieve pain. It encouraged me to study trigger point release and other pain relief techniques.

If you decide to take insurance cases, you need to have a good billing system in place. Decide how often you will do your billing, whether it will be after each session, weekly, monthly or what.

You need to keep very detailed records and keep track of:

- The date of each session
- The date you bill
- The date you receive payment and the amount
- All details on the client's complaints and their progress

If this case goes to court, your records could be subpoenaed. Take notes after each session and keep them in a folder with your client's information.

Disadvantages of Liability Insurance Billing

Unfortunately, it doesn't always work this simply. There are many things that can complicate this process and it is possible for you to bill for many sessions you've done with months going by without getting paid.

I discovered after doing this for a while that I cannot tolerate having money owed to me. In the beginning it seemed great because I could get a lot of work. A client would contact me after a car accident and want to come in regularly for massage for a muscle strain or other injury. The client wasn't paying because it was covered by insurance so they were happy to come in twice a week! Afterwards I had the task of billing the auto insurance company to get paid. There would be an agent to whom I sent the bills. One of these times when I was owed a lot of money, I kept calling my contact at the company and wasn't getting a reply. This was very frustrating, to say the least. Eventually I found out that the person no longer worked there. I don't know what they did with my case. It took me a long time to find someone at the company who could research the case and I could finally get paid.

When I had bills due and I was waiting for checks to arrive at random intervals, it drove me crazy. Since the clients weren't paying for the massages themselves, they didn't seem to take them very seriously. I had one person come in with a book under his arm. After he got on the table he opened the book and began reading, thinking he could read his novel while I worked on him. I felt insulted.

An attorney once called me to ask if I would see a client of his who had been in an accident, promising that the suit would be settled within a month. I was flattered to be chosen, had faith that the attorney was telling me the truth, and agreed to see his client. After two years of waiting for payment, I turned the case over to a collection agency. It was too stressful for me to keep calling the attorney's office. Eventually I received a check for half of the amount of money I had earned. The other half went to the collection agency.

I found myself developing a negative attitude toward clients who paid via their insurance companies. So I had to stop doing it.

If you have a client who was in a collision and is waiting for a lawsuit to be resolved, you could wait years to get paid for your services.

You don't need to bill insurance companies in order to succeed. If, however, you find a system for insurance billing that works for you, by all means, go for it. I know people who do a fair amount of insurance work and make good money from it. Just be sure that your system tracks the dates when you submit billings, the outstanding balance, and payments received. Set up reminders to follow up on bills you have submitted, so you know if you need to re-submit them or contact someone at the company.

Billing Medical Insurance Companies

Billing health insurance companies for massage is different than billing liability insurance companies that primarily deal with accidents. There is, of course, a much wider range of reasons a person will want to use your services.

The laws that govern the scope of a massage therapists' role in providing health care vary from state to state. Some states recognize you as a health care provider and some don't. Massage can generally be covered by insurance when performed under the auspices of a recognized health care provider, such as a medical doctor, chiropractor or physical therapist. In those cases, the work is done as a service that they are supervising, and they are doing the billing. When you are performing the service on your own premises, you need to know what the laws are in your state and what the particular insurance carrier covers.

AMTA on Third Party Insurance Reimbursement

On the AMTA (American Massage Therapy Association) website they have the following article on this topic, written by Susan Rosen, who is currently AMTA's representative to the American Medical Association's (AMA's) Current Procedural Terminology (CPT) Health Care Professional's Advisory Committee.

What are some of the most important things massage therapists should know before considering insurance reimbursement?

Health care is a moving landscape, and it's easy to get intimidated. In order to continue to advance our profession, we, as massage therapists, need to be willing to be part of the larger health care conversation. In Washington state, where I practice, massage therapists are recognized as health care providers, but we still have a choice as to whether or not we bill insurance companies for our services. And just like every state handles the licensing of massage therapists differently, each insurance company handles billing and reimbursement differently. Massage therapists should first educate themselves about insurance reimbursement before determining if it can be beneficial to their practice.

How do individual states' massage therapy practice laws influence whether a massage therapist can bill for insurance reimbursement?

A state's massage therapy board (or other governing board) determines whether a specific procedure or service is within a massage therapist's scope of practice. Even though a state allows a massage therapist to perform a specific procedure or service, it does not guarantee that the therapist will be reimbursed for the service. This is determined by the client's insurance coverage, and if the specific insurance company reimburses massage therapists for their services. For more information, contact your state's massage practice board.

How do massage therapists find out if their clients have coverage for massage therapy services?

Ideally, massage therapists should have their clients contact their health insurance companies before an appointment and ask if a massage therapy benefit is included in their coverage. The client should also confirm that the therapy can be performed by a massage therapist.

Some insurance companies may have massage therapy included in plans as a "wellness benefit." If this is the case, the insurance company might then contract with a massage therapist at a reduced rate and also refer clients to the massage therapist. These clients pay out of pocket but at a reduced rate.

What are CPT codes and who develops them?

CPT stands for Current Procedural Terminology. The codes describe specific procedures and services performed by physicians and health care providers. They represent the standard terminology used to bill for insurance reimbursement. The AMA forms committees to develop and review the CPT codes. As AMTA's CPT representative, I participate in and discuss issues related to CPT codes that impact massage therapists

What are the specific CPT codes that massage therapists can use?

These are some of the CPT codes commonly used by massage therapists; some are used more commonly than others.

- CPT Code 97124
- CPT Code 97140
- CPT Code 97112
- CPT Codes 97010
- CPT Codes 97110

For further clarification on these CPT codes, please refer to American Medical Association. CPT, Professional Edition, 2014, under the heading of Physical Medicine and Rehabilitation, Modalities and Therapeutic Procedures.

Before billing the insurance company, massage therapists should first confirm they are eligible providers and also confirm which codes the company reimburses. Usually a prescription from a referring doctor is required to verify medical necessity.

Massage therapy services are also covered under personal injury protection (PIP) through auto insurance, which is separate from health insurance coverage.

Where can a therapist find forms for insurance billing? Are there companies that will handle insurance billing?

Insurance reimbursement forms can be found through health insurance websites. For electronic billing, refer to OneHealthPort.com. Alternatively, there are companies that will complete and submit all required insurance billing paperwork. (end of article)

Credit Cards

Although it's not absolutely necessary, it's a good business practice to accept credit cards. More and more, people are not carrying cash or checkbooks and rely on being able to use credit and ATM cards. "Square" makes it easy to do with an interface that attaches to your smart phone. You can find them at square.com. PayPal also has a credit card reader that is portable and easy to use with your phone.

Both of these companies have a little device that you can plug into your smart phone that swipes the card, performs the transaction and records receipts that you can email to your customer and keep for your records. A genius invention! This is one more thing that makes your services more accessible and easy for your clients. And think about someone spontaneously wanting to purchase a gift certificate or take advantage of your special rate for a series of massages. If all they did was stop by the ATM and withdraw enough for their one massage that day they would not be able to follow through on their impulse purchase.

Make Money, Pay Taxes, Retire Securely

I mentioned credit cards to Brenda, who was just starting up her practice.

"But then I will have to report the income!" she exclaimed. I sighed, as this is one more way I see massage therapists keep themselves from truly becoming successful business people.

They think "Oh my God, if I make money I will have to pay taxes!"

I have heard this so many times and I have seen this mentality keep people from taking the steps to have a healthy income. All I have to say to that is, "Make money! Pay taxes!" First of all, there are lots of write-offs that keep the taxable amount pretty small. Second, when it becomes time to collect social security, you will be glad you paid into it. It's not going to be a whole lot of fun to turn 66 or 67 and discover that you only will collect $300 per month because you avoided paying taxes all your life. In fact, go one step further and open an IRA and sock a bunch of tax free money away. Look into a SEP IRA, as well. These IRAs for self-employed people don't have as low a cap on yearly contributions. Think how good you will feel when you have put a substantial amount away for your future. With the help of suggestions from some of my business savvy clients I found mutual funds that did socially responsible investing so I could feel good about the money I was putting away.

Go ahead. Take those credit cards and fill your practice!

A Note about Cash Flow

In this business, as in most businesses, you will have times of feast and times of famine in the beginning. One week you won't have enough hours to see everyone who wants to come in, and the next week you'll be sitting around reading the paper and waiting for the phone to ring or texts to come in (checking your phone every so often, just to make sure there's still a battery charge left).

The inconsistency of cash flow can be very challenging. A common mistake people make is to use credit cards when they don't have money, in the hopes they will be able to pay them off when they are busy. My advice is to never count your chickens before they hatch, and to always have a month's expenses on reserve in savings. Finance writer Suze Orman recommends having six months expenses in savings.

This may seem impossible. Often, when you have a busy week and make a fat deposit at the bank after a long period of deprivation, your first impulse is to head to the mall and treat yourself. I know. I've done that. I've gotten high on a surplus of money and gone on great indulgence sprees, only to plunge back into a period of lack when things slow down again or when I get too many unexpected cancellations. It's a terrible yo-yo that can put you in a chronic state of scarcity. It's dangerous to let this cycle get started. If you become fearful about money, you may start viewing your clients in terms of the money they can bring you instead of the energy exchange of healing that is more to the point.

If you always have some money set aside as a financial cushion, you will always feel abundant. Start out by just putting a small amount away. Anything you can manage, just to get it started. Eventually, it will build to a sizable amount.

Of course, there will be times when you need to dip into your cushion and it becomes depleted. If that happens, you must be vigilant about replacing it before making any discretionary expenditures. I cannot emphasize enough how important this is. I have seen many massage therapists who barely get by because they are living at the mercy of this feast-or-famine scenario. Others who are more vigilant about making sure they always have some savings are enjoying their careers and feeling abundant.

My colleague Diana would put all the money she received from the sale of gift certificates into a savings account and did not spend it until the gift certificates were redeemed. Of course some people never use their gift certificates, but in that case the money would still be there and after sufficient time went by she could safely spend it, so in essence it would become part of her cushion.

Being self-employed takes a different set of discipline than having a job. You have to set your own work hours and keep them. You have to make commitments to do advertising, marketing, bookkeeping, and office cleaning. And you have to manage your money. These are skills and practices that you can develop. It helps to have written plans, goals and schedules so that you can keep on track.

It's incredibly rewarding to know that you have succeeded in your own practice. I would not have it any other way. But you must make sure that you have the self-control to take precautions and ride out the waves, for there will certainly be highs and lows.

Sleepy?

Are you yawning right about now with all this talk about money, record keeping and investing? Wanting to close this book and head to the nearest coffee shop for a mocha latte and zone out to Facebook?

Hang in there. Once you get all of this organized it will be done. Your business will work seamlessly and you will be glad you took the time to set it up right. You only have to do this once.

Appointment Calendar

Before you can set up your appointment calendar, you must decide what days and hours you are going to work. It is tempting to want to accommodate people and be available whenever a paying client wants to see you. This is especially true in the beginning when you need the work. You must limit yourself to a set schedule that you can stick to comfortably. Eventually your clientele will fit themselves into your hours.

As far as your availability and setting up your work hours goes, it is good to have some evening appointments as well as some appointments available on weekends, so people who work on weekdays can get in to see you.

It is also very important to have regular days off, particularly two days in a row.

Some sample schedules of office hours are:

Schedule #1

Tuesday:	9:00-12:00 and 3:00-6:00
Wednesday:	12:00-3:00 and 5:00-8:00
Thursday:	9:00-12:00 and 3:00-6:00
Friday:	12:00-3:00 and 5:00-8:00
Saturday:	9:00-12:00 and 1:00-3:00

This is a good schedule for someone who likes to take a long break in the middle of the day, to have a leisurely lunch, do some errands, take care of personal business, or work out at the gym. For some people this helps them recharge their batteries, so they have the stamina to see five or six clients in a day. This weekly schedule allows for 29 hours in the office, which you can divide into session time with breaks in between.

It gives a variety of daytime, evening and weekend appointments to accommodate most schedules.

Schedule #2

Monday - Thursday:	3:00-9:00
Friday:	9:00-3:00

This schedule assumes that most of the business will be in the evenings after the conventional workday. It is also a schedule for someone who prefers to come in and get all the work done at once and have the early part of the day free for other things. This person is also clear that they don't want to work on weekends, and having many week-night hours will alleviate this need. It allows 30 hours in your office.

Schedule #3

Tuesday:	9:00-3:00
Wednesday:	3:00-9:00
Thursday:	9:00-3:00
Friday:	3:00-9:00
Saturday:	9:00-1:00

This schedule does have some early Saturday hours, but the day ends early enough to have most of the weekend free. It alternates between early days and late days, accommodating a variety of clients, and giving the therapist a large amount of personal time each day. It gives you 28 hours in your office.

Many therapists do not schedule a lunch break, because they figure since every available hour won't be booked, they can eat during their downtime. Any of the above schedules would work. It is mainly a matter of preference and managing your energy and time. You also want to consider how much time to allow between clients. Fifteen minutes? Half an hour? There is always a certain amount of time spent schmoozing with your clients before and after appointments. This is part of the relationship, part of the connection of getting to know your clients. Whereas some people are busy and have to rush off when they're done, many will want to spend time talking to you.

The best process for appointments is having an online appointment book that your clients can access whenever it's convenient for them. That way people can make last minute appointments if you have an opening. They don't have to wait for you to get back to them when they call and the process can work seamlessly without taking up your time. Of course, this won't appeal to everybody. You will have people that will prefer to call or text or email, but as much as possible try to steer people to the online appointment book because it will free you up and make things work easier. Most of these online appointment services will automatically send out email reminders for you, which are very helpful. Vagaro.com is a very good one that I know people have been happy with. Another is Schedulicity.com. Several massage therapists I know use that one, as well. A Google search will yield several results. I make suggestions here for those people who find lots of choices confusing and prefer having a good recommendation. I am not in any way aligned businesswise or otherwise with the companies I suggest. I'm just giving you the resources to make it easy for you if you don't feel like doing your own research.

The next step after you decide what hours you are going to work is how much you are going to charge. Will you offer massages of varied lengths (half-hour, hour, hour-and-a-half), or will they all be the same length?

When I first began, I just did one-hour massages. Later on, I added half-hour and hour-and-a-half massages. I highly recommend that you offer a choice.

The half-hour massage is good for people who:

- Are new and want a minimal commitment to try it out
- Don't have a lot of money and want something affordable
- Are interested in purchasing a gift certificate for an inexpensive present
- Need frequent visits to work on a specific injury

This inexpensive means of getting some massage work greatly broadens your ability to reach people. The cost of a half-hour massage is much easier for people to make a decision about, especially if they are not familiar with massage. Often clients will decide to upgrade to longer massages, but this is a good way to get their foot in the door.

An hour is generally the standard for a full body massage for relaxation and relief of muscle tension. The majority of your clients will probably opt for the hour as maintenance for their personal care. A 90-minute massage is recommended when someone needs more focused work in a specific area in addition to wanting a full body massage. Some people prefer the longer massage and will choose that if it is an option. It works best to have that range. Offer a variety and see what people choose and why.

Fees

Setting fees is fairly simple. Find out how much other people are charging in your area and decide where you fit in terms of your own experience and expertise. If you are newly out of massage school, you would charge at the lower end of the going rate. If you have had several years of experience, and especially if you have additional training in specialties, you can justify a higher fee. The most important thing is to not sell yourself short. You will not be more successful if your service is the cheapest massage in town. Another important thing is to avoid the temptation to offer deep discounts, such as two-for-one, half-price, or other eye-catching deals. You are not competing with WalMart. You are a professional.

Although I will be talking in detail about advertising in the next chapter, since we are discussing fees I want to say something about Groupon, Living Social, Amazon Local, and other similar offers. I receive daily emails from these companies that include deals to see massage therapists. My recommendation is not to do this. Why? First of all, you will only receive one quarter of your fee. The advertising company asks you to offer your services for half price and then they take half of that. It doesn't leave you very much and often they will sell quite of few of these so you will be booked up and working for one quarter of your fee. It is possible to limit the amount that they sell, but people often get excited about how successful it is and sell a lot and then they end up working hard for a very small amount of money. You may think this is a good way to introduce yourself to new people, but for the most part, the people who come in with these coupons are looking for deals. They most likely will not come back and pay your normal rate. There will always be someone else they can go to cheaply on Groupon. Promoting yourself in this way cheapens you and your service. You deserve better. Really.

A woman I know, Sandy, told me she was seeing a massage therapist she found on Groupon. She complained about how messy and unappealing the massage room was and how she wasn't all that crazy about the repetitive strokes the woman used over and over.

"But it's so cheap!" she exclaimed.

Yeah. Okay. That about says it all.

Client Records

There are two types of client records: your current clients (within the past two years), and a mailing list of past clients, who have not come in for a couple years.

Your file of current clients could be on a computer or on a mobile device. At the very least, you want to have a record of:

- The client's name
- Email address
- Phone number
- Dates when the client came in
- Any chronic problem
- Notes on what you did
- Specific likes and dislikes

An email list allows you to send out announcements and updates. In an upcoming chapter, I will talk about the benefit of sending out a regular email newsletter.

Intake Sheet

You need to have an intake sheet for your clients to fill out when they first come in. This will give you their personal information, including physical or emotional problems that may have motivated them to come in for massage, as well as any additional information that may pertain to the massage—injuries, chronic pain, specific complaints, and so on. See the sample intake sheet below.

Name _____

Email _____

Address _____

City _____ **State** _____ **Zip** _____

Phone_____ **Date of birth** __/__/__

Alternate Phone Number_____

Do you have a specific complaint you want me to focus on? If so, please explain below.

_____

_____

_____

Have you had any injuries or surgeries that will affect this massage? Anything else I should know?

_____

_____

_____

Is this your first massage?

_____

How did you hear about my services?

_____

Please give 24 hours notice of cancellation, or 50% of my fee will be charged for the time reserved.

I have read the above and I accept financial responsibility for the appointments I make.

_____

Signature

I want to comment on the end of the form that refers to proper notice of cancellation. The client's signature does not give you any legal weight in collecting fees for missed appointments. It is often difficult to collect money for an appointment when the client has not shown up. Occasionally, a client will pay you for a missed appointment the next time they come in.

The main benefit to having a clause like the one above, on your intake sheet, is to let your client know that you are serious about the time that you set aside for them. Once they sign this statement, they are less likely to leave you hanging.

I have rarely asked a client to pay for a missed session. If it is a good client, they often had a valid reason for missing the appointment, such as stuck in traffic, emergency with a child, car wouldn't start, etc. There are some people who have poor memories and will just forget that they made an appointment with you. When I had someone who missed an appointment due to forgetfulness more than once, I would suggest to them that rather than set up an appointment in advance, they try their luck at calling me at the last minute, when they are ready to come in. This has worked surprisingly well. It cut down on my resentment and loss of income from being stood up, and still gives these people a way to get in. For many people, calling at the spur of the moment works best. This is another advantage of the online scheduling system—it makes it very easy for people to get appointments right away when they have the impulse.

Good record keeping is essential to the success of a business. As your practice grows, you will make adjustments to your record keeping so it evolves with you. It is worth the time it takes to set up these detailed records so that you can find information when you need it. This is frequently an area that gets very little attention, as most people would rather spend time developing their clientele or their service than setting up good records. My advice is to do a good job in the beginning. The initial structure only needs to be done once, and it will then serve you well.

The Essence of Chapter Four

- Set up good records to keep track of income and tax deductible expenses.
- Get set up to take credit cards.
- Work out an appointment schedule that works well for your lifestyle
- Create client records to keep track of everything pertinent

CHAPTER 5: MARKETING TO NEW CLIENTS

Now that we have set the foundation for your business, we can talk about marketing your services. Most of the massage therapists I know tend to be sensitive people who love working with clients one-to-one, but are not crazy about promoting themselves. Rest assured, there are many different ways to market your work. You will be most successful doing things that suit your personality and your personal style. Marketing can be an avenue for your creativity. It can be fun. So please bear with me as I discuss different things you can do. Figure out which strategies feel natural and suit your personality.

I have divided marketing into two categories. This chapter is marketing to new clients. The next chapter is marketing to the clients you already have. Both are necessary for you to stay busy. In my mind I have always thought of these practices as "external marketing" for new people and "internal marketing" with the people who already know you.

Consistency = Success

The biggest mistake I see people make with marketing is that they're inconsistent. The great thing about being your own boss is that there's no one to tell you what to do. That can also be the pitfall. Even in your own style, at your own pace, this is still a job that has to be done. Whether your practice is busy or slow, marketing needs to continue. People can see your name around town for years before they decide that today's the day to give you a call. Just like you put money away in case your car breaks down, you need to continue marketing even when you're busy and booked solid. The day will come when a client moves across country, has a schedule change with a new job, or just stops coming—creating an immediate need for you to find new clients.

People's lives change a lot and the most regular of clients could suddenly disappear because of circumstances that have altered their lives. It's essential to consistently put your name and information out where people will see it. New people need to hear about you, and those who haven't been in for a while will remember you.

Marketing Resources

You need some basic materials to give people information about what you have to offer.

Create these:

- Business cards

- A website
- Brochures
- Stationery

We talked about style in the chapter on presentation. Your marketing materials convey your style and personality and give people information about you. It's okay to start out with something pretty basic that you can upgrade and change when you're ready to invest in more complex artwork for a logo and the artistic design of your materials.

Barter Clubs

Don't underestimate the power of bartering for these services. Massage lends itself perfectly to exchanging work with other entrepreneurs. Graphic designers, web designers, marketing coaches and other people who specialize in skills that you need to help you get your business started are frequently open to trade. I found people who were happy to swap services with me for all of these things. There are even barter organizations that make it easy to find other people with whom to exchange services.

You can find information about bartering for services through barternews.com. Or you can search for barter exchanges in your area. Some are nationwide and some are small and local. For several years, I was a member of one called "Trade Services," which only operated in my county. The way it worked was fairly simple. I became a member and had a free profile where I offered my massage services. When I massaged another member of the club, I was paid in "trade credits." I then could spend my credits with any other member of the club. This is a great boost to a new business because it's one more way to expose yourself to new clients. Many people came in who probably would not have spent money treating themselves to massage. Most of the members were in the early years of their businesses. Very soon, I accumulated hundreds of "trade credits" each month. I used my credits on dentistry, restaurants, a graphic designer, car repair, and other specialties. Sometimes I splurged and went to a flower shop that was a member, where I would get $30 of sweet peas and fill my home with their beauty. The dentist I went to became my permanent dentist until he retired many years later. I gained many clients through this club, and long after I ended my membership, they continued to see me.

At any rate, I will share with you some inexpensive resources to get started. This is something you can always build on.

Business Cards

The business card should have your name, title or business name, business address, email address, website, business phone number, and a logo, if you have one. There are many ways to get them done. Vistaprint is an online service that has very affordable cards. You can either use one of their designs or submit your own. Business cards are not very expensive, and they make an impression on people, just as your office does. You can also print them out yourself by purchasing the cardstock at an office supply store. You can buy them in sheets where they are already divided into business cards. Get borderless card stock, which doesn't show any perforations. The borderless card stock is usually set up for eight cards per sheet, whereas the perforated kind is usually set up for ten per sheet. This is a good way to go if you want to just print out a few, are experimenting with card designs, or just need some cards to use while you are figuring out your logo or permanent style.

Your Website

Having a website is essential—particularly for new clients. This is how they will get a sense of who you are and decide whether they want to contact you. The web is the first place people turn when they are looking for something. Or they may have been given your name, but need your address or phone number. Also, people are constantly moving and changing residence. Thus, you have newcomers continually coming to your area, looking for all the goods and services they were used to getting in their last home.

If you know someone who is technically savvy, see if you can trade massages for a website. My husband built me a site because he is in that field and he built sites for several of my massage therapist friends who traded with him.

The most important thing is that your website be easy to navigate and have all the pertinent information. Otherwise, people will only stay for a few seconds and move on. Make sure it is appealing, with good graphics. Remember, people will be searching the web looking for someone who "sounds" good. What can you say about yourself that will sound good? Prospective customers are looking for someone who is competent, experienced, and an expert. If you have been in the field for a while, mention your years of experience. On the home page, have something about your philosophy of holistic health, or something that identifies you as unique. People respond much better to someone that sounds real and sincere than words that sound like marketing. Ask clients to write testimonials that you can put on your website. Your home page could even begin with a quote from one of those. I also recommend having your photo there so people can picture you. Perhaps, even have a photo of you in your massage space. Stay away from stock photos for this, as they will make you seem generic.

You can get a domain inexpensively from a company such as namecheap.com or namiac.com. That way you can have people come to KevinSmithMassage.com. This costs around $10 per year, more or less.

Another very important feature of your website is Search Engine Optimization (SEO). This has to do with people who do Google searches being able to find you. For example, someone who is looking for massage and searches for Massage + Your City is hoping a bunch of local practitioners will come up in this search. In order for this to happen, you have to have the words "massage" and the name of your city in significant places. Either in your domain name—your URL (the name of your website)—or in a page title or a section title. You can also buy several domain names and have them all directed to one website. A web professional can do this for you. That way you can use the words "massage and the name of your town" in a domain name that will help new people find you. There are also tags a web designer can put in that are hidden from view but found by search engines. If you are working with a website creator, ask for these things specifically. Tell them that when someone searches on massage and the name of your town that you want your website to pop up.

Your website should have:

- **Home Page:** Includes your photo, some description of your bodywork, and maybe your philosophy about health or something that makes you unique.
- **Services:** Include your rates. These can be changed easily.
- **About:** A page that tells people about you. This can either be in the first person or third person. A photo is essential.
- **Schedule**: Links to your online appointment scheduler.
- **Gift Certificates:** There are several ways these can be purchased through your website

There are many companies that offer websites for very low fees, where they give you a template and you pop in the content, writing the text and adding your photos. Vistaprint.com, which offers business cards also has website services for a low monthly fee. HostBaby.com is another company with reasonable rates. Also, check out WordPress websites, which are free or low cost, depending on what you choose. You can do a search on "inexpensive websites for small businesses" and see what you find. Basically, they are giving you the template for free and making their money by hosting your site, which is $20-$30 per month, or sometimes cheaper at an annual rate. Google searches on this process will yield a lot of information. But if it seems overwhelming to do all of this research, just go with one of the companies I've mentioned and you will be fine. You really only need something simple so people can find you.

If you want to get a little fancier, your website can be something that is interactive and constantly changing. For instance, if you have a blog and create regular posts you can encourage people to comment and create an online community. That may or may not fit your personality. Find the ways of marketing that suits you.

For stock photos to dress up your website, Fotolia.com has photos you can buy pretty inexpensively. Shutterstock is another, but they are a little more expensive. If you use photos, make sure they look real and natural. I've seen many massage photos that are obviously shot with models wearing tons of makeup, smiling towards the camera and they look completely fake. Beware of using a photo you find via Google Images that you can just drag onto your desktop. If this is a professional photo that you are using without permission, the company who owns the rights to it can come after you with a lawsuit. I have known people to whom this has happened. It's horrible. Make sure any photos you use are legitimate.

There are also photos that are available to use for free called Creative Commons. These are photos that have been made available for other people to use at no cost. Flickr and other sites have Creative Commons photos. Sometimes all that is needed is giving credit to the person who owns the photo.

If you want people to be able to order gift certificates online, you can set up an account with PayPal so that people pay you, and then you manually mail them their certificates. It's very easy to set up. Go to PayPal and click on the Business tab and follow the instructions to accept PayPal payments. Customers can send you money via PayPal simply by using the email address you use to set up your PayPal account. You don't need a shopping cart on your website for this, which is an unnecessary expense. The customer can send you an email through the Contact Page on your website, ordering the gift certificate and pay you using PayPal. You will receive an email from PayPal that the payment has been received and then you can mail the individual the gift certificate. PayPal will make a direct deposit into your bank account. If you email the gift certificate, give it a code so it can't be used twice.

Make sure your website is mobile friendly so it looks good on a phone or tablet. The technical word for this is "responsive."

Brochures

It is helpful to have something to hand people when you are making personal contact. Although your website will have all of this information, if you meet someone somewhere and hand them your business card, going to your website involves extra steps. If you have a brochure to hand them they can immediately see what you have to offer.

Standard brochures are the three-panel variety. A brochure can give more information about you, where you went to school, the type of bodywork you do and what your specialties are. Include a picture (very important) so your new clients can see you. Have testimonials from clients you have helped on one of the brochure's panels.

Prices for your work are optional. Whereas you can easily change the rates on your website, you don't want to have to print up new brochures if you change your fees and you still have 200 brochures left.

There are many situations where having a brochure is helpful. I attached a brochure holder to the outside of the door to my office. That way, people wandering by when I was closed or in session could pick up a brochure to take home with them.

It's a valuable tool. I have also had them handy when I made friends with another business owner or healing arts practitioner who was interested in referring clients to me. Many businesses would let me leave a few in their reception areas, as well.

Stationery

You will be surprised how often you will have an opportunity to use stationery in your business. I have outlined several strategies later in this chapter for direct mail that require using nice stationery. Anytime you do a mailing to another professional, you want to use stationery. If you mail someone a gift certificate, you ought to enclose a note with it and you'll need stationery to do that.

If you are thanking someone for a referral, use your stationery to send them a note and enclose a gift certificate for $10 towards their next session.

Nice stationery, with your logo or at least your business name, address, and phone number on high quality paper makes a positive impression. In fact, since people use email for most communication these days, using quality stationery to do a mailing for a specific purpose will make you stand out.

Getting Your Name Out There

So how will they know you are there? You can be the best massage therapist in town, but if no one knows about you, you won't have a massage practice. Although word of mouth is the best form of advertising, you have to massage a lot of people before that really starts working for you. Consider that only perhaps ten to twenty percent of the people who are referred to you actually come in, and you will realize that you need a large referral base before you can rely much on word of mouth. That is why you want to continue to do things that keep your name out there. Someone may be referred to you by a friend or by someone in the healing arts and not get around to contacting you, but then they see your name pop up somewhere else and it reminds them. Getting the word out is pivotal to your success.

Marketing Budget

In the beginning of your practice, plan on spending a sizable amount on promotion in order to get started. Later, you will work out a maintenance amount that fits with your general budget for operating expenses. But in the first few months of your new practice, a good chunk of money should be earmarked for advertising as part of your startup costs. I suggest that for the first three to six months of your business, plan on spending four times the amount that you will spend as a maintenance budget. For example, if your long-term plan allows $150/month for marketing, begin by spending $600 a month for a while—at least three months, and if possible, the first year.

Advertising

Many of the things I am about to tell you will have minimal cost. The more effort you throw out into the world, however, the faster you will attract clients, and the quicker your practice will fill up. Ads are the most expensive thing you are likely to do, whether in a publication or online. You may want to consider local journals that focus on highlights of your area, such as entertainment, art, music, and events. Although expensive, these ads reach thousands of people. If your ad is attractive and appealing, you will get attention. The more you advertise and the more people who see your name, the more people will come in for appointments. If you don't spend money on ads, your practice will take longer to build. If you prefer to spend less and take your time, you can just do the less expensive networking methods I suggest.

I advertised in our local newspaper on the movie page when I first opened my practice. I did a package with them where I advertised every week for a year for a special annual rate. I gained many clients that way. It was absolutely worth it for the first year. Afterwards, I stuck to less expensive methods.

If you do create a display ad, consider using a photograph of yourself. With personal services, it is very helpful for your prospective client to see you. Most publications will put the ad together for you if you give them the basic information. Give them a good photo (something natural looking—not like a photographer took it in a studio, but more relaxed and friendly), your logo if you have one, and just a few choice words about your practice.

From Chair (Massage) To Table

Doing chair massage in the workplace is an excellent way to meet new clients and make money while you're doing it. If you have a client who works somewhere that might be appropriate to have someone come in once a week to do chair massage, suggest that to them and see if they can make an introduction for you. If you don't have a connection like that, make up a handout that describes what you offer, and then go around to some of the sizeable companies to see if any of them would be interested. You will be surprised how many think it's a great idea. Relaxation breaks during the workday have been known to boost productivity. Generally, you can do about three 15-minute sessions in an hour, so charge accordingly.

High tech companies, sizeable medical offices, legal firms and many other industries have welcomed chair massage in the workplace.

Leslie is a massage therapist who has a client who works in the administration department of a local hospital. Her client talked to the staff about having Leslie come in once a week to massage the hospital employees. She began by coming in on Friday afternoons. This became so popular, it extended to the full day, once a week. She gets many clients who have come in to see her in her office after initially getting a chair massage.

The staff pay for their own massages, although one year the hospital bought 120 chair massage gift certificates to give out to personnel for the holidays.

Carolyn has a client who owns a travel agency. She has Carolyn come in once every two weeks to give her staff chair massages. In this case, the client pays Carolyn to massage her staff as an employee benefit.

Personalized Direct Mail

Sending out an introductory letter to prospective clients is a great way to build a practice. Although this costs money in printing and postage, it can be a great way to get new clients in the door. Even if you move to a town where you don't know a soul, you can build a practice this way.

Buy a mailing list of people who live within a 5- or 10-mile radius of your office to whom you can mail a letter telling them about your services. On the internet, search "residential mailing lists by zip code" and see what comes up. One site that sells targeted mailing lists is leadsplease.com, where you can purchase 500 names for $50. You can select the criteria. For example, I would suggest choosing people aged 35 and over, who are homeowners in a zip code that has high-end real estate. This ensures you will be mailing to people who can afford your services.

I am constantly surprised by people who tell me that they don't know where to go for a good massage. Perhaps they got a massage while on vacation at a resort and want to continue to get treatments when they come home, but don't know where to begin. They may see advertisements from massage establishments and the idea of getting a massage may appeal to them, but they don't know if it will be any good. There is a lot of trepidation about getting a massage from a stranger, so you have to find a way to build a sense of trust with the people who you haven't yet met.

What they need is a personal connection. You can give that to them in a well done mailing piece. I did a lot of this during my first five years. I regularly sent out direct mail pieces, and I got some of my best clients from them. Direct mail has three major advantages. It is relatively inexpensive, you can enclose a lot of information, and if done properly, it will get their attention and be opened.

The piece that you send out should convey the message that you are a person of quality who is looking for high-quality clients. You can do that by the letter you write, the way that you express yourself, and the great care with which you create your mailing. This is why I recommend that you have high quality stationery. If you don't already have letterhead and matching envelopes with your name, your business name, and your logo, then get some printed. Use good paper, such as 60# linen or some other type of textured paper that will immediately make the envelope from you stand out from the rest of their mail. Since the people opening these letters don't know you, every little detail will make an impression on them that will either encourage them to contact you or cause them to throw it away.

Clients won't know if you really give a good massage until they come in. All you can do is appear convincing enough for them to give you a chance and try out your services.

You can make the mailing personal by using their name when you write the letter. It takes a little more time to use the person's name and then copy and paste the rest of the letter but it's worth it. To ensure that your mail gets opened, hand address them with blue ink and inside, sign the letter by hand. Trust me. This works.

Your mailing should include a letter introducing yourself and telling the prospective client about your services, including the benefits they will receive after having a session. People unfamiliar with massage need to learn more about why it can make a difference for them. You should include a brochure, or at least a menu or description of what you offer, and a business card that includes your web address so that it's easy for them to refer you to others. If you don't have a brochure, this may be a good time to design one.

If you only offer one service, or if your work is a combination of everything you've learned that you use intuitively as needed, then write a detailed description of how you do that. You don't need a menu of services. The most important thing is to give the prospect a sense of what their experience will be like when they come in to see you, and how they will feel when they leave. If writing is not your forte, get a friend who's a good writer to create a juicy description of your bodywork.

If you don't feel ready to create a brochure right now, you can include all the pertinent information about your bodywork in the letter you write. If so, a letter describing your work and a business card will suffice. Just make sure that the letter is not too long. People aren't likely to read something that is more than one page.

Here is a Sample Letter

Dear _____,

My name is _____ and this letter is to introduce myself to you. I just opened my massage office in your neighborhood. I have been practicing bodywork for _____ years. My specialties are _____. The advantage of this kind of work is_____.

As I am building my clientele, I am offering new clients $20 off your first visit so you can come in and see how you can benefit from my professional massage services.

Please use the enclosed coupon when you come in. I have included a price list and description of my services. If you have any questions, please give me a call or make an appointment using the online scheduler on my website. I look forward to meeting you and contributing to your health and well-being.

Thank you,

_____

Of course, this is just a brief draft to get you started. Make it personal. Make it welcoming and friendly. Let your expertise show.

Either you can offer a lower price as an introductory offer, or you can offer an extra fifteen complimentary minutes if they pay your usual price. The advantage of the latter is that they get used to paying your regular rate and they don't get in the mindset of only being interested when you are offering a discount. For example, you can offer your standard hour massage with an additional fifteen minutes of foot reflexology or extra time in a special area of focus. Or you can offer your standard hour massage with a fifteen minute scalp and facial treatment. You get the idea. This is another way of reaching people you would otherwise not have access to.

It's so rare for people to receive something personal in the mail like this that many will respond to it because they will be curious about meeting someone who has taken the time to create it. People are really bombarded by ads online and in social media as well as plenty of "junk" mail, and they will find this quite refreshing.

It does take time to write and print out letters and address envelopes, so plan on spending a certain amount of time each week working on this. This is an excellent way to spend down time when you're having a slow day, which you will in the beginning. Once people start responding you will see how rewarding it is.

When I first started my practice, I made a commitment to send out 100 letters per week. I got a mailing list of 1000 names and gradually went through it. When I used them all up, I bought more. It came with mailing labels but, as I said, I hand-addressed the letters instead. It gave me something productive to do when days were quiet rather than fret about being slow. I was introduced to such wonderful people this way, whom I otherwise would never have met. They were impressed by the sincerity and personal touch of my letter. Once they came in, they loved my work and the way I had set up my office. They were happy to have found me. I got many new clients who came regularly, referred friends, and bought gift certificates. I bought lists of people in neighborhoods where homes were expensive, so I knew the recipients could afford my services if they felt sufficiently compelled to try me out.

A few months after your first letter goes out, you can send a similar letter to the same mailing list. Repetition is essential in advertising. Some people will see the mailing the first time and think about your offer, but will not get around to doing anything about it. However, when it comes around a second, or even a third time, they will respond.

Networking with Other Professionals

This direct mail process also works well for connecting with professionals who are in a position to refer people to you. If there is a particular group of people you would like to reach—such as chiropractors, psychotherapists, or medical doctors—you can create a direct-mail piece specifically targeted to them and send it out. Do the same method of personalizing it and hand-addressing the envelope. You can buy lists of professionals in your area from these mailing list companies, or you can simply do web searches. If you conduct a search on professional organizations, you can find a whole list of people in a specific category in your location. This makes the process easy and free. You can do the same thing with email, but if people don't know you it's very likely that your piece will just go into their spam folder. Since these are people with whom you want to set up a relationship to get referrals, let them know that in your letter. Offer them a free massage to try out your services. Enclose a gift certificate for them to use.

Sample Networking Letter

Dear _____,

My name is _____, and I am a massage therapist, writing to make your acquaintance. Massage has many health benefits, and I'd like you to be aware of my work for those times when it may be helpful for your clients (patients). I have been practicing bodywork for _____ years. My specialties are _____.

I have enclosed a gift certificate for you to use so you can experience my work personally. I am interested in learning about your work as well.

If you have any questions, please give me a call or make an appointment using the online scheduler on my website. I look forward to meeting you.

Thank you,

_____

Networking in Person

This is more effective than mailing because you will make a personal connection right away. Pay attention to the offices and businesses near you and identify which ones might be good referral sources.

These are:

- Salons
- Health clubs
- Yoga teachers
- Physical therapists
- Doctors
- Acupuncturists
- Psychotherapists
- Counselors
- Personal trainers
- Other people in the healing arts

When you walk in the door and speak to the person at the front desk, be upfront with them about your intentions. Let them know that as a way of promoting your services, you want to introduce yourself to people who can refer to you. Tell them that there's no obligation, that you just want them to experience your work so that they know you and what you do. Most of these people, if not all, are self-employed themselves and they will completely understand what you're doing. You'll find that many of them will want to help you. Once they come in, let them know that for every person, or two people, or three people (your choice) that they send your way, they will receive a free massage. I have a friend who started her practice in a very small town and she built her entire business this way.

This has many advantages. You will form relationships with other people in your community where you will be mutually supporting each other, since you will be referring people to them as well. You will make new friends. Some of these business owners will have other ideas for you on how you can promote yourself.

For example, imagine that there is a health club near your office. Go in and ask if there is a personal trainer you can talk to. There is. His name is Jim. Just one moment, please and he'll be right with you.

A few minutes later, a friendly-looking, smiling man who is very buff and who keeps wiping his hair out of his eyes comes over to you, thinking that you are possibly a prospective client. You put out your hand.

"Hi Jim, I'm Molly. I came in here to introduce myself because I have a massage studio a couple blocks from here and I wanted to meet other people in the health field so we could get to know each other and cross-refer. I would love to give you a complimentary massage so you could have a firsthand experience with what I do. I brought you a gift certificate, which is good for the next month...so please come in and use it. What kind of training do you do?"

There you have it, the beginning of a conversation. It's important to have a gift certificate or coupon with an expiration date so the person has something to exchange for the massage. Just leaving them a business card is unlikely to be effective. Time will pass and they will forget to use it. If they remember later on down the road, it will feel awkward to assume they can still get a free massage. But a coupon or certificate with an expiration date in a month is much more likely to bring them in now.

Mary Ann, a massage therapist in Michigan, recently contacted me and mentioned that she has been approaching referral sources and they seem interested when she talks to them and hands them one of her business cards. She offers them a free session to try out her services, but then they don't call for an appointment. She was frustrated, asking me why this was not working. Let's explore why this may not be working for her.

Picture this scenario. What if you are a yoga teacher at a yoga studio. A massage therapist comes in and tells you he is spreading the word about his services and he'd like you to come in for a free massage so you can tell your students.

Sounds great, right? The therapist hands you his card and perhaps a brochure and leaves. Maybe a month or two goes by and you come across the card. You wonder if he's still offering free massages. It feels a little awkward now to call up and expect a costly service for free. You shrug your shoulders and decide not to call.

Now imagine instead that he gives you a coupon or gift certificate for a complementary massage that expires in a month. You have something in hand to exchange for the massage. You know you need to get in there before the offer expires.

If you are not comfortable approaching people directly, send them something in the mail. Make it personal and from your heart so that they get a sense of you as a real person. This may be a bit slower because you won't have direct face-to-face contact with them, but people will still respond to your mailings. Always use a handwritten envelope and sign your introduction letter by hand. If this is the extent to which you feel comfortable, do work on building up your courage to approach people more directly. (Listen to the recording I made for you. It will help. See the section on guided visualization.) If it feels too awkward to walk into someone's shop or office to simply introduce yourself, patronize them. Use their services and get to know them and let the connection build that way. Once I realized how open and friendly other professionals were to me, I became more confident about approaching people.

This strategy not only introduces you to new people who can refer clients to you, but it keeps you busy doing massage, practicing your skills, and staying in touch with your work.

Keep some coupons or gift certificates with you all the time because you never know when you might meet someone who would be a possible referral source and a good person to reach out to. You can leave the expiration date blank and then fill it in when you hand it out.

In addition, some people can feel uncomfortable taking an offer of something that's free because then they feel obligated—and you want them to refer people because you're AWSESOME, not because they feel obliged. Your coupon can be for a free half hour so they can experience your work, and you can enclose a note with it saying that they can add to it and have a longer session, if they want. That way, if they are concerned about taking advantage of you, they can instead get a discounted massage. Or they still have the option of getting half an hour for free, if they wish.

More Categories of People To Approach for Referrals

In addition to the obvious people in the health and fitness fields, there are other people who would be interested in knowing about you.

I found that realtors make very good clients. When a realtor sells a house, they get a hefty commission and often want to treat themselves to something. I had many clients who were in real estate and would come in to reward themselves after a home had sold. In addition to treating themselves, they often bought gift certificates for the buyer. It is a common practice for a realtor to give a client a housewarming gift when they sell them a house. My realtor gave us a set of locally crafted wind chimes. A massage is a fabulous gift to give someone who just bought a house and exhausted themselves with a big move. You may want to do a targeted mailing to realtors, or stop by their offices and make a personal connection.

Another group of people worth contacting is those in the hospitality industry. If there are bed and breakfasts nearby or small hotels, they are also good people to meet and to give your brochures and a gift certificate. They are also in a position to refer to you. Buy a nice brochure holder and see if they will let you put a stack of brochures in their reception area. If you can get them in for a massage (with a gift certificate that has an expiration date) and turn them into a fan, they will happily recommend you.

Packages that Combine Your Services with others

Once you start making friends with other businesses near your office, see who may offer things that you can combine to create a special package for people. For instance, there was a salon near my office that specialized in organic facials. They used a line of luscious natural skin care products and some blends that the owner made herself. I love facials, so I would patronize her whenever I could afford to. I talked to her about offering a combined package of my services and hers, and she thought it was a great idea. That way we were both able to sell massage/facial packages to our clientele. The package included gift certificates for massage and a facial, as well as one of her products. We kept track of the certificates by numbering them. When I sold a package, I paid her for the portion that was hers. She did the same with me. It was a very popular gift for birthdays, holidays, anniversaries, and Mother's Day, and it brought in business both to my new friend and me. This way we both benefited and were able to expand the services we offered without actually expanding our businesses.

This worked so well that for the entire month of May, I offered a Mother's Day special where a woman could come in, get a massage, and then get a skin care treatment around the corner. This was extremely popular. At one point a sweet little bakery cafe opened and I had the idea to include lunch as part of the gift. I talked to the owner and he agreed to participate, so a gift certificate from the cafe was added to the package.

I wanted to have something similar that I could offer for male clients, but I didn't think that many of them would go for facials. There was a sporting goods store in a neighboring shopping center and one day I got up the courage to talk to the owner and see if he would be open to me selling gift certificates to his store combined with a massage for Father's Day, birthdays, and holidays. He thought it was a fabulous idea!

He then came in for a massage and became a regular client. This was very successful, and yet, it had taken me a while to get up the nerve to ask him.

I then wrote up a piece about the two types of combination packages, and had that as a handout for clients. At holiday time and for Mother's Day and Father's Day, I wrote about it in my monthly newsletter, sharing details about the other businesses I was working with.

People love gifts that combine a number of things. This is also a great way to make friends with neighboring businesses, and to help them prosper along with you.

More Combinations of Services

Perhaps there is a yoga studio nearby where you can work out some sort of package with massage and yoga classes. That way the yoga instructor is promoting you while you're also promoting their classes.

Mutually beneficial arrangements like this are the best!

You can get together with a chiropractor or acupuncturist and offer a wellness package that includes a session with each of you. These packages don't just have to be gift ideas. The wellness combinations, in particular, can be something that clients can do where they receive a discount by buying the package of services.

Offer to design the card that describes the special. The other health professionals will really appreciate you. Your energy and enthusiasm are infectious.

These are opportunities to be creative and make new friends. Other entrepreneurs are always happy to meet people who will help them with promotion as everyone runs out of ideas and appreciates new input. It's always more fun if you're teaming up with someone else.

And if you run into someone who doesn't respond positively to you, just shrug your shoulders and move on. You will find the right people. Do trust that you will attract colleagues and clients that will be very happy to have found you.

The Essence of Chapter Five

- Create your marketing materials: website, business cards, brochures and quality stationery
- Create a good website that is a comprehensive resource for people who want to know more about you.
- Be consistent with your marketing. Create a plan where you devote a certain number of hours per week, or a certain number of tasks to promoting yourself.
- Personalized direct mailings can connect you with people in your neighborhood that will become loyal clients.
- You can use direct mail to network with other professionals who will refer to you.

- Getting to know other complementary businesses in your neighborhood can help you form referral networks and build strong alliances.
- Creating packages with other complementary businesses can be very popular and profitable for all of you.

CHAPTER 6: MARKETING TO CURRENT CLIENTS

Once clients start coming in to see you, they will fall into a number of different categories. Many will come sporadically when they get the craving for a massage, which could be anything from weekly to annually. There are those who will seek you out only when they have a specific complaint. Your core, however, will be the ones who keep regular, scheduled appointments with you. The ideal is to have at least half of your appointment calendar filled with people you see on a consistent basis.

Strategies for Helping Clients Come in Regularly

The secret to having a stable practice is to have your clients get in the habit of coming in as part of a routine and booking their subsequent appointment each time before they leave. That way your calendar will always be partially full with people whom you see regularly.

I have outlined four strategies for encouraging regular appointments. It's a good idea to offer several options because it gives people a choice and it makes it easier for them to choose something if you have something printed up. Different options appeal to different people, so give them a choice that feels good to them.

- Give a discount for keeping a standing appointment. For example, when a client books their next appointment before leaving and keeps that appointment, they get a discount—maybe $5 or $10 off. You can put a symbol or code next to their name, and if they cancel or change the appointment, that code will be erased. But if they come in and the code is there, they booked ahead and they get the discount. It is the easiest and most successful method. They don't have to lay out a lot of money, and they get in a regular massage habit. This is the most effective option of the four.

- Offer a pre-paid package, such as six massages for the price of five. The client is paying ahead, so you get paid in advance and your client gets a great deal. You can let them use their package to treat a friend or partner, or to buy a gift certificate, and they will go through them pretty quickly. So, it might look like this: If your rate is $80 per hour (I'm using California prices, prices may differ in other parts of the country), your client pays $400 for a package of six, or $66 per massage. Big savings! You can sell a lot of these during the holidays, and you will be surprised how many people will choose to do this ongoing.

- Offer a bigger package, such as eleven massages for the price of eight. Your client pays $640 for a package of eleven massages, or $58 per massage. Even though you are getting a lot less from the people who purchase packages, it gives you a measure of security, and you are still getting full price from people who book one at a time. If the people who purchase packages use some of those as gift certificates, it will also increase your client base.

- Give clients a frequency or punch card that you mark off each time, offering them a free massage after they come in 10 times, or half price after coming in 5 times.

Selling a block of massages gives you a chunk of money right away. But if your client doesn't come in frequently, you aren't building that long-term habit. In the long run you want people who will have a standing appointment that they keep for years and years—and you know how much more people benefit from a regular massage than just getting one occasionally.

Create a handout describing your frequency program that you can share with your clients when they come in to see you.

This is something you can also post on your website, as well as send out in an emailed e-newsletter.

Say to them, "I'm offering some really good deals to help people get in the habit of getting regular massage. It's so much more effective that way, and it gives you something to look forward to. People are responding really well to this." Then hand them your printed piece. You can go over it verbally, if you want. Encourage them to book their next appointment before they leave so they can get a discount next time. You don't have to be pushy. This is a very simple strategy that sells itself. You're just making it easy for people to take care of themselves.

I used to sell a block of six massages for the price of five. Often a client would share the massages with a partner and use one or two for a gift certificate. These six massages were used up in no time.

Monthly E-newsletters

E-newsletters are a great way to stay in touch with your clients. It keeps your name in front of people who already know you and are familiar with your work.

Set up an email list using something like MailChimp, a free online service that enables you to send out mass emails easily with all sorts of formatting choices. It has many templates that you can customize for your mailings. It allows you to keep multiple mailing lists so you can have lists of current clients, a separate mailing list of clients you haven't seen for a year, and any number of other categories of lists you may want. It also will give you feedback about how many of the emails you sent were actually opened, which is great feedback for you.

Your mailings can include seasonal specials and reminders to buy gift certificates for holidays, such as Christmas, Valentine's Day, and Mother's and Father's Day. You may also want to inform your clients of any changes that take place, such as a special course you take, a new service you are offering, or a product that you are selling. It is good to stay in touch with your clients by email on a regular basis, in order to keep your name in front of them.

I used to send out a monthly e-newsletter where I would write about things that I found to be beneficial for good health that I wanted to share with my clients. They were like blog entries that I mailed out to people. Sometimes I had a special to offer. Sometimes I just sent out the e-newsletter filled with my own philosophical meanderings about how to live a more relaxed life. These pieces reflected my personality and often would inspire conversations when clients came in for their sessions.

I recommend that your e-newsletter have more than specials so they become something worth reading. Use them as an opportunity to share things of interest, such as ways of stretching or a movement routine that can help keep your body free of tension. You could even entertain your clients with humorous pieces about stress and mindfulness that have a spiritual perspective. An email that consists of nothing but a bunch of specials is boring. You want to be fun. So write about something personal. Give a few examples of good health practices from your life, especially anecdotes that include funny stories so that your emails are enjoyable to read as well as having good deals in them.

Remember, having a business is an opportunity to be creative. Put your whole self into it. If you have been practicing Buddhism or a type of meditation, let people know about it. Tell them about whatever new thing you're doing that is helping you have a better life. Your clients will look to you as someone who has some answers about living a better life, not just massage therapy.

In many ways, your clients will see you as a role model. They will view you, not only as a massage therapist, but as someone who can help them with many aspects of their health. This includes having a positive attitude, which, as you know, is as important as what you do physically.

People will be attracted to you because of who you are. Sure, some people will decide you're not their cup of tea. But many more will want you to be an essential part of their life. Be your quirky self. Let your business glow from your colorful personality. The world is increasingly full of chains and big corporations, and this goes for spas as well. People are hungry for interesting individuals, and a truly personal connection.

There is plenty of room for you to show who you are, and from your unique being, you will develop a long-term, faithful following.

If writing is not something that comes naturally to you, consider sharing excerpts of articles that you come across— just make sure you give credit to the source (e-zines, website) and the author. You can also have links to books that you'd like to recommend or even movies. The nice thing about e-newsletters is that it's easy to insert photos and you can turn them into links. This way, it's easy to share information with your followers.

Not only is an e-newsletter good for promoting your services, but it is a good way for your clients to get to know you better. The more that they "bond" to you, the more loyal they will become and will refer the people in their own spheres of influence.

Interestingly, it will also encourage you to take better care of yourself. You'll find that you'll be evaluating a lot of the things you do as potentially share-worthy. When you find something new that has a highly beneficial effect, you'll store that away for another e-newsletter topic. Keep a notepad on your phone where you can jot down ideas as they come to you.

Social Media

Utilizing social media is better for staying in touch with people who already know you than for seeking new clients.

That said, people may share or retweet something you say, so it can be an opportunity to get a referral or recommendation.

Facebook

In addition to your own website, you can reach out to people through Facebook with a business page. Again, this is probably a better approach for keeping your current clients interested rather than a way of getting a lot of new people— although it is another way for word of mouth to be effective. In general, people on Facebook are not interested in businesses who are constantly marketing to them. They may "like" your page, but if all they get from you are solicitations to patronize you, they might, in turn, keep you invisible so your posts don't show up. You can link to your website from Facebook, and you can activate a button on your timeline that links people to your scheduling software with a call-to-action button that says "book now." Other than that, use this mainly as an opportunity to share meaningful things, and let your fans get to know you in a more personal way. This will help them connect to you more deeply. It's kind of similar to the e-newsletter, but a much briefer format.

Unlike an emailed e-newsletter, which will go to your complete list, Facebook does not show your posts to everyone who has liked your page. When you post, that post will pop up in the newsfeed of a fraction of your followers. They use complicated algorithms to decide who gets to see what. They try to show people things they think they want to see. If people have liked, commented on, or shared your posts in the past, they are likely to show them new posts. If you post about a subject they have responded to, even from someone else, they may be shown your post. If you want to be sure your followers see all your posts, you can boost them. When you hit the "boost" button, it will give you several options for targeting your post. For as little as $5 or $10, you can pay to have your post boosted to "people who liked your page." This is worth doing.

You may want to use your Facebook business page to share articles on health, relaxation, and anything that pertains to the type of practice you are creating. Vary what you share between informative posts, entertaining and inspiring posts, and reasons for people to make an appointment with you. Also, if you want people to share content from your Facebook business page with their friends, post something humorous. I have had a greater reach from posting silly humor than almost anything else. People also enjoy things that are inspiring and give them new ideas. That is the best use of social media. Create an emotional connection.

Twitter

Twitter is another good method for engaging people. It can be a fun way to stay connected to your followers and keep interest going through frequent tweets. The main purpose of Twitter for Business is to let people know you exist and stay in their minds. I recommend this for those of you who have fun posting tweets. This is another way to share more of yourself with people and another opportunity for others to spread the word about you by re-tweeting and favoriting your tweets. It's mainly a way of engaging with people and having a good time. Twitter is a place where you can let your personality shine and create an audience. If it's something you enjoy, you will develop a pool of fans.

Twitter is also a great way to network.

Linked-In

Setting up a profile on Linked-In is a good way to have a presence on this business-oriented social media platform. The nice thing about Linked-In is that once you have your profile set up, you don't need to spend time maintaining it like you do with Facebook and Twitter. People who have heard of you and want to find more information about you before giving you a call may do some research online. When they see you have a Linked-In page, it shows them you take what you're doing seriously. It's like a resume that has your education, skills, and achievements.

Instagram

You can use Instagram for your massage business by posting photos that pertain to your business as well as from your personal life. It's another way for your followers to get to know you. The website, socialmediaexaminer.com, has a great section on using Instagram for business. You can link your

Instagram account to your Facebook page, and have images show up in both places. Videos can be posted there, too. If photography is an art form you like to play with, this is a good venue to share your art with your clients and greater community.

In general, find the social media platforms you enjoy and have fun with your posts. It's not necessary to do everything under the sun to promote your business. All you really need to do is find one or two things to focus on and work on creating engaging posts.

Let Your Personality Shine

Lisa, a massage therapist with a full time practice, is a big proponent of raw foods. She studied them at a health institute and learned they are chock full of enzymes and make a big difference in promoting good health. She used a raw diet at one point in her life to heal herself of chronic fatigue, and so she has personal experience with the benefits of this diet. She tries to eat 80% of her diet raw. Of course, she enthusiastically shares this information with her clients. She even makes snacks—a type of raw cookie made in a food dehydrator that she serves clients with a cup of tea after their massage. Her clients love learning about this from her.

Carrie studied Bach Flower Remedies, which are homeopathic essences that help balance moods. The founder, Edward Bach, believed that illness stemmed from negative states of mind, so he spent his life researching the effects that various plants essences had on emotion and how they could affect different personality types. Carrie found this fascinating, experimented with the essences on herself and eventually took certified courses in using them. She shares this with her clients and puts together combinations for them when they request it.

Share the healing modalities that interest you with your clients. If there's a writer you really like, or a spiritual teacher, share their wisdom with your people. There are many people who are hungry to know more about how they can live in a healthier, more satisfying way, and they will view you as an example. Without being pushy, you can share those things that have made a difference in your life.

Andy is a therapist in Southern California who has great self-deprecating humor. He uses humor to lighten the mood, even when talking about very serious issues. In this way, he makes it easy for others to share their vulnerabilities. This is the sort of thing that makes people feel especially safe and comfortable. His clients see Andy as someone with whom they can really let their hair down with and be themselves.

People frequently don't really know what draws them to a particular massage therapist. More often than not, someone will say that they just like the way it feels to see a particular bodyworker. They are speaking of this subtle persona.

Reviews

Once you have developed a good relationship with a client, ask if they would be willing to write a review for you on Yelp. Some therapists also have a section of reviews on their websites. These are extremely valuable. People have become accustomed to reading reviews about everything they purchase and they will appreciate being able to read reviews about what a great experience your clients have had with you. Don't be shy. People are used to getting requests for reviews, and your fans will be happy to write one for you. Just send them an email with a link to you on Yelp and ask for the review.

You can use quotes from these on your website and in your brochure.

All of this does take time, so please be patient with the process. If you follow these guidelines and remain persistent with your marketing plan, you will have a solid practice that will support you for as long as you want.

The Essence of Chapter Six

- Present a variety of ways clients can save money by coming in regularly.
- Send out a monthly e-newsletter that not only contains specials, but also contains small articles about healthful things you believe in. Make them personal.

- Choose some social media platforms that appeal to you and post regularly as a way of sharing more information and staying in people's minds

- Map out a marketing plan for the year, breaking it down monthly and weekly. Narrow down your efforts into bite-sized, manageable pieces.

- Reviews are very beneficial in helping new clients feel comfortable contacting you. Request a review from your loyal followers.

CHAPTER 7: MAKE A MARKETING PLAN

Success comes from steady, focused marketing that is carefully planned and executed. Business promotion tends to be something that we think about when things are slow and we need new clients, whereas we can easily fall into a state where we ignore it when we're busy. But the reality is that many marketing efforts can take months or years to kick in. Someone gets a mailing from you and doesn't get around to calling until she sees it for the third time. Another person drives by your office every day but doesn't really notice you until she sees your brochure on the counter at her yoga class and makes the connection. Referrals that come from relationships you make in the community will happen randomly throughout the year, often many months later. The thing with marketing is that you need to have a series of tasks that you keep up on a regular basis because they will spark and catch fire at various, unpredictable times.

Sit down and map out a strategy that details what you're going to do for the coming year, in terms of advertising, social media, mailings, etc. Write down everything you want to accomplish. Then break it down, month by month so that you have a clear idea each week what you are working on.

Then, at the beginning of the week, look at your schedule and set aside time each day when you can get the tasks done.

For example, if you want to create a Facebook Business page, decide which day will be devoted to that. Block off half a day to research the process and then do the page set up. There is a lot of information on how to do Facebook business pages, both on Facebook and by searching the web. It may take several sessions to get it the way you want it. You can always change the artwork, the description—basically everything. Once you have the basic page created, decide how many times per week you want to post and start to collect things that you think will be interesting to your fans. It's helpful to have a folder or a notepad on your phone to put ideas as they come to you. The posts can be scheduled in advance, so you can actually create several posts at once and schedule them to run on different days through the week. In the block where you put your Facebook post, if you click on the button in the lower right corner that says "publish" a small menu drops down and one of the items is "schedule." If you click on it, a calendar pops up whereby you can choose the date and time your post will go live. This way you can set up posts for the entire week in one sitting.

If you want to do a mailing campaign, like the ones I outlined for prospective clients or to meet people who could make referrals to you, organize time for those tasks around your client schedule. You can break it down into small pieces. One block of time will be for addressing fifty envelopes. The next period can be for printing out the letters. The third bit will be for stuffing the envelopes and ta da, they are ready to mail. Dividing this into small, simple tasks makes it easy. You can have everything ready to go and then plan to do some of it each day, during an hour or two when you have no clients scheduled.

Figure out each week what project you're doing to promote your business. That way you have a plan, knowing that there's something you are doing on a consistent, regular basis to help your business grow. Marketing can seem really daunting at first, but when you break it down into small pieces like this, it becomes manageable.

In the beginning, you may not know how long a particular task is going to take. After you have done a little bit, you will get a sense of how many hours to devote to each project. Once you start doing this, it will become part of your regular routine just like doing your laundry, paying your bills and doing your shopping.

MAKE A MARKETING PLAN   125

A Sample Marketing Plan

For the coming year:

- Mail introduction letter to 2400 residents
- Mail intro letter + gift certificate to 300 referral sources
- Create Facebook page and post 2-3x per week
- Create Business Twitter account and post daily
- Monthly e-newsletter
- Create networking group
- Do two chair massage events

To give you an idea of what this might look like on a daily/weekly basis, I've mapped out a schedule to illustrate what I'm talking about. Since a lot of this stuff may feel boring, or at least not what you really want to do, I suggest following the tasks with treats as a reward for getting them completed. That's often how I will cajole myself into getting work done that I don't really feel like doing. It works!

Tuesday

9:00 - 9:45	Address twenty-five envelopes
10:00 - 10:30	Get a mocha latte and read news
11:00-12:15	Massage client
12:15-2:00	Have lunch, then go for a walk around the lake
2:00-2:45	Address twenty-five envelopes
2:45 - 3:00	Do stretches to music
3:00 - 6:45	Massage three clients

Wednesday

11:00	Print out fifty letters
12:00 - 2:30	Massage two clients
2:30 - 3:30	Stuff fifty envelopes. Have a cup of hot chocolate
3:30 - 4:30	Mail envelopes and go for a walk
5:00 - 8:45	Massage three clients

Thursday

9:00 - 10:15	Massage client
10:00 - 11:00	Write draft of monthly e-newsletter
11:00 - 12:15	Massage client
12:15 - 1:00	Finalize e-newsletter, find a good photo and set it up with MailChimp, send to list
1:00 - 3:00	Meet a friend for a nice lunch and a walk in the park
3:00 - 6:45	Massage three clients
7:00	Treat yourself to a yummy dinner

Friday

12:00 - 1:15	Massage client
1:15 - 2:00	Choose three things to use for Facebook posts and schedule the posts over the next week
2:00 - 3:15	Massage client
3:15 - 4:00	Get some frozen yogurt and go for a walk
4:00 - 5:00	Run some errands

| 5:00 - 8:45 | Massage three clients |

Saturday

10:00 - 12:30	Massage two clients
12:30 - 1:00	Have a quick lunch
1:00 - 3:30	Massage two clients
6:00	Meet a colleague for dinner and to brainstorm about networking and supporting each other.

This is an example to show you how you can fit it all in. In this hypothetical week you saw twenty-three massage clients, allowing for 15-minute transitions in between them, got your marketing done, made some social connections and still had plenty of personal time, including two full days off where you were not working. Every week will be a little different. If you are aware of your goals and have a list of what you want to get done, you'll be able to squeeze in the marketing work (and of course the treats and rewards) around your massage schedule.

Begin your week by deciding what items on your to-do list you are going to accomplish and then figure out each day where you can squeeze that in around your client schedule. It will start to become routine.

It's very important to have your objectives written out so you can organize your projects and create a timeline. Understandably, things will change as you get new ideas and opportunities come up. The important thing is that you are consistently making concrete efforts to promote your work. Certain things like the monthly e-newsletter and Facebook posts have to happen on a regular basis so your people get in the habit of hearing from you. After a while, you will get into a groove with your business promotion. You'll figure out shortcuts. You may even be able to trade massage with someone who can do some of the work for you, like addressing envelopes. Think of the marketing for your business as though you are feeding your dreams. These tasks are the food.

Getting your marketing done will give you a great sense of accomplishment. It is especially rewarding when clients who come in to see you tell you that it was getting your e-newsletter or seeing your Facebook post that reminded them they were due for a massage. Or when you get new, wonderful clients from the results of your introductory mailings to local residents.

Remember that your advertising efforts are an opportunity to be creative and put your own personal ambience in the community. Whether it is your website, business card, blog, Google ad, or monthly e-newsletter, everything that represents your business in public is a reflection on you and your business persona. Have fun with it. Let the flavor of your unique style of doing things be part of how you present yourself to people when you tell them about the bodywork that you do. For example, some people are very involved in sports, movement, healing, preventing injuries, or a particular health or spiritual practice. Share your excitement about these things. Let your clients know what you do to take care of yourself. Invite them to have conversations with you about the healthy things you and they engage in.

My background in psychology and hypnosis flavors much of what I share with clients. I find it interesting what psychological things make us feel good or make us feel stressed, and I'm always looking for new approaches to life so we can change negative patterns. These are the sorts of things that I would write about in my e-newsletters. If you go to my Facebook page or read my blog posts, you'll see what I'm talking about.

Marketing from a down to earth place where you share the things that matter to you is very powerful. Enjoy it!

The Essence of Chapter Seven

- Make a marketing plan for the year, including all the things you want to accomplish.
- Map out a monthly strategy, deciding what you want to do each month.
- At the beginning of each week, decide what you're going to get done and work those tasks around your client schedule.
- Be consistent, continuing to market your business whether you are busy or slow.

CHAPTER 8: GIVING CLIENTS THEIR FIRST MASSAGE

Once your great reputation gets around, you will begin to get referrals. People will want their friends, relatives, and co-workers to experience your wonderful hands. Your clients will purchase gift certificates for the people in their circle. New people will respond to your efforts to reach out into the community and make yourself known. Sooner or later, you will find yourself giving a new client their first massage. Although you probably gave people their first massages when you were in school and practicing on friends, it's a very different experience when you are set up in your office and meeting people for the first time.

Earlier in this book, we talked about the importance of setting up a professional environment. This is especially critical with new people. Upon your first introduction, it's essential for you to establish right away that you are a professional with whom they can feel confident.

When it's Your Client's First Massage with You

Although you will have people fill out an intake form, you will also learn a lot from your initial conversation with them. Always ask new clients if they have had a massage before. If they have, see if they can tell you what they liked or disliked about it. I have had clients with previous bad experiences decide to give massage a second chance. This was a big responsibility. Always listen very carefully. Find out as much as you can about what they disliked about the previous massage. Was it something about the therapist's personality? Their style of bodywork? The environment in which they practiced? Your clients will teach you so much about what is good and bad about the profession by what they say.

When it's Your Client's First Massage Ever

If a new client has never had a massage before, you need to make that person feel safe. The best way to do this is to begin by describing what will happen. As much as you can, change the unknown into the known. Let the client know that although it's important to get undressed, a sheet or blanket will cover most of their body. Tell your client that you will check periodically to see if the pressure is right and if you have found the right spot. Although you don't want to chatter through the whole massage, some talking in the beginning is important in establishing rapport. If you have had the client fill out an intake form, check to see if there are injuries or chronic problems. Be aware that many people won't know how to tell you what they want. They might be afraid to ask. Sometimes they won't even know, but being attentive and giving them a positive experience will bring them back.

Once you have told your new client a little bit about the massage, leave the room to afford some privacy for undressing. Let your client know that removing underwear is optional—many people feel more comfortable leaving it on the first time. Make your client feel at ease by helping them get comfortable on the table, making any necessary adjustments with the headrest, bolster and pillows. And be sure to tell them where the bathroom is.

Remember when you got your first massage? What were your fears? What about your hopes? What did you wish your massage therapist had done or said? How do you feel when a doctor examines you—especially someone you don't know? Doesn't it help when procedures are explained to you first?

Many first-time clients will be full of questions. What is the purpose of that stroke? Why do I hurt there? What does it mean that my bones click every time I move like this? What is it about your technique that makes the pain go away? What causes the pain?

Sometimes you might wish that the client would just be quiet and enjoy the massage. But really, your client is asking to know that everything's okay, that he or she is not the most difficult person you have ever worked on, that you know what you're doing, and you've got things under control—that it's safe to relax.

Clients come with many hidden needs that you may or may not be able to meet through a massage. Your hands can help, but they cannot remove all the pain from people's lives. You can, however, help them change the way they experience themselves. You can help to transform their energy and effect a powerful change in their emotions and attitude. This is not trivial. Helping people really let go can certainly change their lives. Once they see that you are not going to do anything threatening, they will begin to trust you and let you in. It may happen during this first session or it may happen over a period of time as they get to know you better.

One suggestion is to avoid the stomach and abdominal area during the first massage. This is especially important if a client seems nervous. The front of the body is where most of our internal organs are. To expose someone's stomach and abdomen will make a person feel vulnerable. I eventually stopped working on the stomach altogether, unless someone had a particular complaint, such as a digestive problem, or asked specifically to have their stomach massaged.

Make your clients feel cozy and snuggly with soft sheets, a well-padded massage table, and a nice, warm massage room. Have an extra blanket available in case they are cold. Heating pads designed for massage tables are a wonderful invention. If they are thirsty, give them something to drink. Make some small talk. Then leave the talking up to them and let them be your guide as to whether they feel more comfortable talking through the massage or being silent.

If your client seems very talkative it may mean they feel an obligation to be social and aren't used to just being quiet and allowing themselves to be cared for. In this case, guide them to breathe slowly. Take over the conversation just enough to encourage them to be quiet and tune inwards. Often they are not sure what is expected of them, and being on the receiving end of this kind of care may feel foreign. Once they understand that you are encouraging them to be quiet and receptive, it will be easier for them to calm down and receive.

The Extremely Tense Client

Sometimes you will encounter a client who is so tense that nothing you do seems to help them relax. Such a person may talk quickly and animatedly throughout the session. Some people's bodies are so armored that they are completely unresponsive to anything you do. In this instance, you need to do something to break through the client's resistance to relaxing.

It helps to have clients do an exercise in which they tighten up as much as possible and then let go. The idea is to exaggerate the tension by clenching so tightly that you actually break through their point of tension, which to them feels normal. After exaggerating the tightness, releasing the tension often leads to a much more relaxed state. You can guide them to do this from head to toe, tensing and releasing each area. For the first time the client will be able to feel the difference between tension and relaxation. You will know it's working when the client becomes quiet and begins breathing slowly. You will feel their muscles soften under your touch. Guiding them to breathe and directing them to imagine breathing into a tight muscle or general abdominal breathing is also very helpful.

Specific Problems

Your client may have made the appointment for the massage because they have a specific complaint. They may be experiencing muscle pain, headaches, back pain, or some other condition they are hoping massage will alleviate. It's important to know your limitations and be very honest with yourself and your client about ways you can help them.

In my early days of practice, I learned the hard way not to work on someone the very day they pull a muscle. I remember very clearly the day a construction worker came in for a massage with a muscle spasm in his back from lifting something too heavy. His back muscles were locked in a tight contraction and causing a lot of pain. I did my very best to massage him and worked hard to loosen up those muscles. Unfortunately, his body reacted by tightening even more. He could barely get up off the table. At the time, I didn't realize that in the first twenty-four hours of an injury, the body is adjusting and responds defensively. It tightens up to form a barrier against any sort of invasion. My lesson was to never massage anyone within the first twenty-four hours of sustaining an injury like this. In talking with a chiropractor who was a friend and colleague of mine about this situation, I learned the R. I. C. E. approach:

- Rest
- Ice
- Compression
- Elevation

The conditions clients who were seeking therapeutic massage came in with inspired me to learn a lot more and expand the depth of my practice. My chiropractor friend told me to study trigger point release, a method that is wonderful for relieving pain due to chronic muscle tension. I did this, and eventually he and I taught workshops on it together. I studied deep tissue therapy, pregnancy massage, myotherapy, and other pain relief techniques as a result of people coming in and needing different kinds of help. It's not necessary to know everything in the beginning. Knowing your limitations is important, too. You have your entire career to take continuing education courses and learn more.

Sometimes someone who has never considered massage before will contact you because they are having a problem and they feel desperate, hoping that massage will be the answer. This is when it's very important to be able to assess them properly and know if you can indeed help them or if you need to refer them to someone else.

When the Massage is Over

After the massage, it is nice to give your client some quiet time to integrate the relaxation. I let the client know that I am done and will be waiting for them out in front, and they can go ahead and dress once they are ready to get up.

When the client comes out, be respectful of the mood they are in. It is nice to give them something to drink to rehydrate and wake up. They may not be feeling talkative. Ask them if they'd like to make another appointment. If they would, schedule it in your appointment book, and then write the date and time down on a business card for them. If you are using an online appointment book, they usually have a feature that will automatically send the client an email when you book the appointment and will send them reminders a few days beforehand.

It is not a good idea to discuss the benefits of massage at this time. Unless the client asks questions, I would keep talking to a minimum. Frequently, people are so relaxed that they are not in a thinking mode and want to walk out with this lovely feeling of bliss. Remember, this is a new experience. They may be relaxed in a way that they have never before experienced. Make sure they are wide awake enough to drive, and let them enjoy their peace.

If you are concerned that people may drift away without making an appointment and will forget to come back, you may want to follow up this first visit with a thank you card or email. Simply thank them for coming in, let them know that you were pleased to meet them, and that you hope they will call for another appointment soon. The reason this is effective is that people are frequently not thinking in an organized manner at the end of a massage, so may not feel like looking through their datebooks. A few days later is a good time for them to reflect back on the wonderful massage they experienced, and then they may be ready to set up a time to do it again.

Giving someone their first massage is quite an honor and a wonderful opportunity for you both.

The Essence of Chapter Eight:

- To put a client who is new to massage at ease, carefully explain as much as you can about the experience.
- Use some simple breathing techniques to guide them to relax, since this kind of treatment may be foreign to them.
- If the client presents a medical condition or specific problem, be aware of what you can help them with and when they should be referred elsewhere.
- Follow up with a thank you note to welcome them to your practice.

CHAPTER 9: SETTING RELATIONSHIP BOUNDARIES WITH CLIENTS

You have a very specific role as a massage therapist with your clients. They are coming to you for help and support, whether it is to relax, get relief from pain, or any number of things that fall under your training. There are appropriate ways for you to behave, parts of your life that are okay for you to share, and things that you should keep to yourself.

As you get to know people better and better over a period of time, they can start to feel like friends. In fact, there may be some people with whom you share common interests and whom you think would be enjoyable to get to know and spend time with outside of the massage setting. A book about setting up a massage practice would not be complete without addressing how to handle situations where people suggest doing other things together beyond your massage appointments. Like any professional, you need to be careful how you handle these interactions, and to be aware of what is appropriate, what to share about yourself, and what to keep private. This chapter goes into detail about several different kinds of personal relationships that people develop with clients, and how to handle them appropriately.

Some people prefer to keep a clear separation between professional and personal relationships, and they have a blanket policy not to see clients outside of the professional context for any reason. In many states, massage therapists are considered licensed healthcare professionals and it is a legal and ethical violation to have personal relationships with clients. It is your responsibility to know and understand the laws in your state.

In some cases, however, you will find that there are gray areas in your relationships.

I'm going to discuss four basic types of personal connections that might come up with your clients and ways to handle them.

☐   People You Know from Other Contexts

☐   Business Relationships

☐   Personal Friendships

☐   Romantic Overtures

People You Know in Other Contexts

Some of your clients will be people you know from other settings. You may get clients who know you from church, from the tennis club, from your child's play group, is your brother's wife's cousin, is your dance teacher, is your accountant....and so on.

Unlike the people who meet you fresh from referrals, the internet, or advertisements, all of these people will have seen you in a different role rather than purely as a healer. It will be necessary to establish that when they come to see you in your office, you take charge as the massage therapist—regardless of whatever hats you may each wear under other circumstances.

There are several things to be aware of that will help your client feel more comfortable with you. Since your client knows you from another world, there may be a tendency to talk about the things you have in common. It is your job to gently help them to relax, and to take control of the environment so that they don't feel obligated to talk and can truly unwind.

One way you can shift gears with them is to talk about the massage. Tell them what you will be doing, just like you would with any new client. Ask them questions related to the session, so they can start to respond the way they would with any massage therapist. If you keep bringing them back to the purpose of the session, they will eventually understand that they can allow you to be the healer. They don't have to keep up a conversation about gardening, hiking trails, or whatever they are used to talking to you about when they see you outside the office.

You may want to use more technical terminology or stay focused on their particular aches or pains to really establish the fact that you are trained and have expertise. It takes a while for people to view you this way when they are used to seeing you in a different context.

Once you are able to show them how much you do know and how much you are able to make a difference for them, they will be among your most loyal clients. The fact that they already know you will give them a deeper sense of trust. They will recommend you to other people with confidence, proud to have you in their circle of friends or acquaintances. The fact that they not only know what quality work you do, but also like you as a person, will make them among your biggest fans.

You will find that when you see them other places and they introduce you to people, unless they want to keep the fact that they are seeing a massage therapist private, they will mention what a great therapist you are, perhaps using themselves as an example of the quality work that you do.

They will say things like, "Hi, I want you to meet Molly. She's a terrific massage therapist. I had terrible back pain until I began going to her. She has magic fingers. My husband has just begun to see her, too, and is getting relief from his chronic headaches." What better advertising can you get than a statement like that?

Business People

Many of your clients will be other self-employed people who come in for a massage after a busy day. Several of the people who had offices in my building came to me for massage. Since we saw each other almost daily, we developed a very comfortable camaraderie. We gave each other referrals, and frequently shared stories of the highs and lows that we experienced being entrepreneurs.

My space was next door to an office that several psychotherapists shared. Linda was one of the therapists whom I got to know pretty well. She came to me for massage several times and occasionally had clients whom she referred to me.

I got to know Shirley, a marketing and business coach who pioneered business events for women in my community. She organized an annual Women In Business Conference and created a directory of local female business owners that she circulated throughout the year. I wanted to be in her directory, so I introduced myself to her and she soon became a regular massage client. I also wanted some help learning the best ways to market my business, and Shirley proposed that we trade massages for business coaching. Eventually we developed a close friendship.

Yoshi owned the Chinese restaurant where I frequently went for lunch and eventually she became my client. I often came in to eat during odd times of the day when my schedule had unfilled hours, and her restaurant was between meals so she had time to sit at my table and visit with me.

There were many other clients who were business people whom I did not see outside of my office, but who had a genuine interest in what I was doing and gave me incredibly valuable advice. I'll never forget a conversation I had one day with Gary, a very successful insurance agent.

"What is the secret to your success?" I asked him.

"Molly," he said, "Persistence is the main thing that has seen me through. I have had a lot of failures, but I've always dusted myself off, picked myself up, and tried something new. And a few of those things have worked out very well."

These are just a few examples. As you can see, you and your business can grow to become a fixture in the community. The fact that we were all small entrepreneurs—part of the same local networking community—gave us something in common, and we provided each other with resources and help when we needed it, as well as good company at other times. Whenever you share your experience and what you know, everybody benefits.

Please remember, however, that while they are on your table, they are there for healing and relaxation. Even if you have an outside business relationship, it is not appropriate to ask them business questions during their massage. Establishing strong boundaries in this way will help you appropriately nurture and honor your relationships.

Personal Friendships

Taking your relationship from a professional/client role into a personal friendship can be tricky. This often evolves naturally, but there are things to be aware of. It is important to remember that sometimes your clients will view you in an idealized manner. They see you not only as someone with massage skills, but as a health professional that serves as a role model. Indeed, you have an opportunity to model a healthy lifestyle that your clients will find appealing. You must realize that they will sometimes view you as way more perfect than any human can possibly be. Part of this is because you are there to serve them, be a comfort to them, be a support person, and to listen to them when they need to unburden themselves. It is not an equal relationship. Whereas it is perfectly fine for a client to come in and complain about problems they are grappling with, it is not at all appropriate for you to discuss your problems with your client.

Clients have made many assumptions about me. They thought I was always in a positive mood. Often I am, but like anybody, I have had my days of doubt. I certainly have had times in my life when I was dealing with tough issues and needed to unburden myself and get support from a friend. But my clients were not the people to do that with, even when they felt like friends. At times when they cared very much about me and asked how I was doing, they were not really coming to hear me process my problems the way I might with a friend. This was their time to unwind.

My clients were interested in all the health practices I did. They were curious about my diet, whether I was a vegetarian or vegan, or if I practiced fasting. They wondered if I did yoga, meditation, or regular exercise. I could tell by the questions they asked me that they viewed me as a role model of healthy living whom they could learn from. They often wanted my input about a specific health regime that they had heard about. I enjoyed being helpful and it encouraged me to learn a lot about a variety of health practices so I could respond intelligently to them.

There were a few people with whom I became pretty comfortable who wanted to extend our connection beyond the office. Sometimes I would meet them for lunch. However, it took me a while to realize that even outside the office I had to be careful because people did not really see me accurately.

For example, I once had a client whom I got to know rather well and whom I sometimes met for meals. Jamie and I were slowing developing a nice friendship. She came from a family who owned several local wineries and happened to be very wealthy. I loved the fact that she knew our area so well and could introduce me to little farms and businesses full of art and culture.

Things were going along just fine until one day while we were eating at an Italian outdoor cafe she asked me if I would like to accompany her on a trip to Southeast Asia. She wanted to travel to Viet Nam, which had become quite a tourist destination. This caught me by surprise. For one thing, a trip like that was way outside my budget. Also, whereas I enjoyed getting together for lunches and to occasionally tour a farm or art gallery, a trip like the one she was suggesting felt like too big a commitment of time to spend together. Although there were many ways we connected and many things we enjoyed talking about, suddenly I was quite aware of being in a very different world and economic bracket from her. At that time I did not have the confidence to explain that to her and instead her suggestion had me feeling awkward. I didn't want to make her feel wrong for inviting me. However, I knew this was something I couldn't even begin to think of doing with her. I'm sure I made up some excuse about not being able to get away. It was a lesson to me about socializing with clients. It was fine to get to know people outside of the office, but I had to be conscious of the fact that there were areas where our lifestyles might clash. I had to be prepared to stay within a context that felt appropriate, where we would both be comfortable.

There was another woman—the wife of one of the doctors who referred patients to me—who became a regular client. Lynn was not someone who fell into a deep, quiet state during the massage, but was very talkative. Indeed, I think part of what she enjoyed was having someone receptive and non-judgmental to talk to. I enjoyed her very much. She had a great sense of humor. We laughed a lot. One day she invited me to join her on a tour of some of the historic homes in the neighborhood. I thought it sounded like fun, so we made plans to go.

Once we started our tour, I made a comment about something using a slang expression, just as I would with one of my friends. Lynn responded by making fun of what I said. This was subtle, but it made me aware that this was not the way she talked and that she didn't really know me. I realized I needed to monitor my way of speaking and my behavior a little more formally than I was used to with personal friends. Again, this was an uncomfortable moment. I did not want to alienate her, but I also did not feel as relaxed with her as I had hoped I would. This was something I had never thought about during our sessions because at those times I was mainly the listener and support person. Although the outing was kind of fun, it was also a bit stressful once I became aware that I could not fully relax and just be myself. It was an important learning experience about accepting offers to get together with clients. I know that part of that had to do with my own expectations. I realized that we could still get together outside of the massage room, but I had to be somewhat on guard and as long as I could adapt to her way of talking and doing things we were fine.

There was another instance where I had a client who was a graphic designer. Janet had a small business working out of her home doing art and design for local companies. She asked if we could trade services, which we did, and she helped me design newsletters, flyers, and ads in exchange for massages. I found this very helpful. With her, the relationship felt more equal. We were around the same age and in a similar economic bracket. We had many of the same interests, and the back and forth flow felt very natural. One day, I was giving her a massage right before the Fourth of July weekend. She asked me what plans I had for the holiday. I told her I was going on a camping trip near Lake Tahoe where a friend of mine had some property, and had invited a whole bunch of people to come up to camp all weekend and celebrate his birthday, which fell right on the holiday. There would be live music, a talent show, and other planned activities. She asked if she could come along. Apparently, she knew some people in the area, didn't have any plans, and wanted something to do. My camping trip appealed to her.

By this time, I had known her for a couple of years and, unlike the previous examples I gave, Janet felt like she would fit right in with my circle of friends.

"I'm leaving right after work today. How soon can you pack?" I asked. She said she'd go home and be ready by the time I got there. I picked her up after work, we went on the four-hour drive into the Sierras, and she and I began a friendship that lasted for many years. As I predicted, she blended right in with my friends.

The important issue here is to distinguish people with whom you can really let down your hair from those with whom you still need to maintain some professional distance even when engaging outside the massage setting. There are many shades of friendship. These relationships are part of your core base of fans who will help promote and support you, and you have to be careful how much you share about yourself once you are outside your office because you don't want to alienate them. Obviously, you will also forge lifelong friendships with people you meet this way. Therefore, you have to really think things through and move gradually before you end up embarrassing yourself or your client. You will be making these sorts of judgment calls throughout your career as you get to know people through your work and theirs, and as each of your relationships grow.

Romantic Overtures

Since massage is a very personal and intimate service, there may be times, particularly if you are single, where your clients may get romantic notions about you. This can happen in any profession. However, it is particularly dangerous in health professions such as massage, psychotherapy, and medicine because you are caring for someone at a time when they are vulnerable and could be in need. Their perception of the situation could be very unrealistic. This is something that we have to be aware of and handle as gracefully as possible.

Projection and Transference

Transference and projection occur when a client imagines you to be the person he or she hopes you are, rather than the person you really are. Your role with your client is that of a fully supportive person—always focusing on their needs, including being a good listener when they want to unburden themselves. You may be seen as eternally sweet, wise, loving, giving, understanding, accepting, tolerant, and possessing infinite patience. It is easy enough to hold these qualities for someone for an hour or two, but this is not the way anyone behaves all the time.

The client's experience is always one of receiving your positive energy without having to give anything in return, other than money and perhaps a few words of appreciation. It is possible for them to build you up in their mind and see you in a way that they invent, even falling in love with you, although they may not be consciously aware of it. Therefore, it is your job to gently keep things on track and carefully remind them, however subtly, that they are there for a professional massage session.

If a client asks you out, you must graciously decline. Dating a client is considered unethical behavior on your part, and you could lose your license because of it.

Counter-transference

Counter-transference has to do with the qualities you imagine your client to have—qualities which may have little to do with reality. Perhaps there is something about the way your client adores you that draws you in and makes you want to be closer to him or her.

Your clients will undoubtedly regard you very highly, but as I discussed earlier, they are not necessarily seeing you realistically. Their vulnerability may appeal to the part of you that needs to be needed, a draw that is very common among people in the healing arts. It's something we have to watch— the way we can get drawn in to people with problems, particularly if they are appealing to us to help them. We thrive on being helpers, and that works fine in the container of the massage session. But if we get to know them outside of the massage context, being in the position of the helper can be very one-sided.

Be careful.

There could be something about your client that pulls you into their drama. If you feel this happening, look inside yourself at areas where you might need to do your own inner work.

Transference and counter-transference are both terms used in the field of psychology to highlight how clients and therapists can get emotionally confused in their relationships with each other, where they don't view each other realistically. These lapses in boundary awareness are all too common. I know people in every field of the healing arts who have crossed this line, and so I say this with the utmost attention to caution. It's important to be aware that this happens so you can observe it, be present, and act appropriately.

General Awareness

Most of the people you massage will remain people you only see when they come in for their appointments. However, being aware of the issues discussed above will help you make wiser decisions when a client suggests getting together for another purpose.

The Essence of Chapter Nine

- It is essential to be aware of your role as massage therapist in every client interaction, and your job to maintain professional boundaries.
- Gently show people whom you know from other contexts that when they come to see you in your office, you are now in the role of their healer rather than however else they know you.
- You will develop a camaraderie with other entrepreneurs in your community, and these will likely develop into varying degrees of personal relationships. It's important to be mindful of who really fits in your personal life and who should stay purely as a business connection.
- There are some clients with whom you may feel inclined to become personal friends. This is fine as long as it's a truly good fit. Otherwise, a clash of different

lifestyles could prove both uncomfortable and could be bad for your business.

- Be careful when a client expresses romantic feelings towards you and be especially on guard if you find yourself emotionally reacting to such overtures. This is not appropriate.

CHAPTER 10: MANAGING YOUR TIME WISELY

Your time is your most precious resource. You can raise your prices to earn more money or increase money with a financial investment, but you have a finite amount of time. Money can be saved up. Time is always passing. It is critical to spend your time wisely and to realize that your time is another boundary that is important to protect. Just like you need to budget your money for expenses, treats, and a retirement plan, your time also needs to be budgeted for both essential and discretionary purposes.

As a massage therapist, your time is what you have to sell. I have often referred to professional services as the commodity of "skilled time." But you will be surprised at how much of your time you give away.

How Time Can Slip Away

Let's say you just finished giving a massage. You don't have another client scheduled for four hours. You are planning to spend the rest of the afternoon going to lunch at your favorite restaurant, shopping for something to wear to an outing this weekend, and getting some essential errands done. You figure your activities will fit into your afternoon break perfectly and get you back to the office in time for your evening client.

But the person who just got up off the table is in no hurry to leave. He is feeling very relaxed, open, and warmly toward you. He begins to talk to you about how good he feels, and about insights he had while getting the massage. Soon he is beginning to move into his philosophy of life. All of this is fascinating, to be sure, but your stomach is rumbling and you are eager to leave and take care of yourself.

Meanwhile, your client is settling in, getting comfortable in your waiting room chair. He has put his sneakers on, but the laces are not yet tied. Every so often he makes a move to bend down and tie one of them, but then he becomes distracted in making a point, forgets what he was doing, and straightens up to face you. By now, you find you have become obsessed with watching those untied laces and waiting for him to reach for his checkbook. It is hard to concentrate on what he is saying. All you want, at this point, is to leave. And in order to do this, he has to leave first.

What Do You Do?

There are both verbal and non-verbal signals you can give your client, to clue him in that it's time for him to get on his way. Some people will literally stay for hours. In my beginning days, I would frequently sit in my office trapped, not knowing how to encourage clients to leave. If I didn't have a client right afterward, which was frequently the case in the beginning, I would end up listening to people for hours, trying to be polite, remembering that this person had paid me money, and feeling helpless about how to get control of my life again. Thus, someone who paid me for an hour would sometimes get two: one hour of massage, and an hour of counseling or chatting. More than once, I took a client to lunch with me because I was desperately hungry and still didn't know how to tell them to leave.

It took me a while, particularly in developing self-confidence, to get control over my time.

In a situation like this, one thing you can do to let the client know the session is over, is to gather up your things as a signal that you are planning to leave when your client does. You may put on your coat, pick up your keys, and finish the transaction in a standing position.

In fact, even if you don't make moves to leave, conducting the transaction in a standing position is a signal for the client to leave—that you have other things to do. Once you sit down, your client will get comfortable and think that this is your choice and that you have nothing else you want to do other than hang out. Clients have no idea about all the things that fill your busy day. They can be completely unaware that there is time-consuming work involved in running a business. They may assume that your massage practice is much simpler than it is. If you don't have another person walking in the door as they are leaving, they probably think you would enjoy having a little company. Of course, it never occurs to them that it's a one-sided relationship, and that it requires effort on your part to be the kind, compassionate listener—always conscious of taking care of their needs and putting your own aside.

If they don't get the non-verbal clues that you are ready to move on to other things, then you need to say to them, "Well, I have to get going. I have several errands I need to do."

Or, "I'd better get moving. I have an appointment at 3:00." Asking when a client would like to reschedule can also be a lead-in to the end of the session.

You can also act as though you do have another client right after them. The way you start moving, needing to get ready for you next person, is automatic when you know you need to keep things moving along. Pretend that this is the case and your client will pick up on your energy and subtle message that they need to leave.

Remember, for many people you are the most healing person they encounter. Your warm, nurturing, caring energy is so pleasant that they will stay and bask in it for as long as you will let them. Sometimes you will have a client who is going through a difficult time and will really need to talk—and you may want to offer your time to them because you do care about them. There may be people with whom you have developed a strong rapport, whom you want to help and give a little extra to. Go ahead, but be selective. The intimate nature of this work draws a lot from you emotionally as well as physically, and if you give too much of yourself away, you will burn out.

When Clients Request Odd Hours

It is best to have a set schedule that defines your work hours. It is important that you don't schedule people all over the map and find that you have no days off, or that you are strung out for hours and hours waiting for people, with long stretches of unproductive time in between. I knew someone who complained of always having clients at each end of the day, with long empty spaces in between. That situation basically kept her from making any plans. It would make much more sense to have six-hour work periods, offering early hours on some days and late hours on others. (see the suggested schedules in Chapter 4)

This also goes for working late or coming in early to accommodate people who can't come at other times. Once in a while, it doesn't hurt to go out of your way for someone. But if you start doing it often, you begin to lose control of your time. You start to feel that none of your time is really yours, especially if it is always subject to being overridden by someone who needs an appointment. You start becoming an unpredictable friend who can only make tentative plans because you could get a phone call from a client at any moment.

The worst case is when you go out of your way to book the client and cancel your other plans—and then the client doesn't show up.

This happened to me a few times when I scheduled people on Sunday, which was my day off. I remember very clearly one time, during my first couple of years in business, when a client called up who really needed a massage. It was already too late in the day on Saturday to fit him in. He asked about Sunday, and although I was very much looking forward to my day off, I made an appointment with him for the middle of the day. Well, of course I was unable to really make any plans that Sunday because I had the appointment. My whole day seemed to revolve around the fact that I had to go to work in the middle of the afternoon.

I went in and he didn't show up. He wasn't a new client. He was someone I had seen several times before and whom I trusted to keep his word. I tried calling him, but there was no response. He probably fully intended to keep the appointment when he made it, but then something else came up and he went off, forgetting all about me and his commitment. I was very frustrated, more at myself and my tendency to give more than was comfortable, than at my client. Although it always makes me irritated when someone doesn't show up for an appointment, it isn't nearly as infuriating as having that happen when you book someone on your day off. Unless the person has paid you in advance, don't do it.

Managing Fear of Scarcity

The problem people run into is their fear of scarcity. They worry that if they can't squeeze that client in somehow, they will lose them.

There is a tendency to fear the loss of a client if they are not able to fit into our regular schedule. Perhaps we will lose them, or at least this week we will. Such is the nature of limitations. Sometimes we have to say "no." Sometimes we have to let them go and call someone else who may have more time available.

I have known people to break dates, cancel parties, miss important events, or give up their day off to be there for a client who can't make it during regular hours.

Letting clients know that you are busy and that you have a life is not going to turn them off.

Part of being able to set boundaries and stick to them requires having the faith that enough people will fit into your work parameters to support you, regardless of whether you have to say "no" to a few of them. You must believe that you will not go out of business by having a set schedule and keeping it. Once you start being motivated by fear, it turns into a downward spiral and you become a slave to your practice. Eventually you'll become wound up with stress because it will be such a chaotic part of your life.

The truth is that people will work with the schedule you set. Let them know what your boundaries are. If you honor them, they will, too. Your clients contend with this with every other professional who is a part of their lives. Their doctors, therapists, accountants, hairdressers, and attorneys all have set hours, and your clients have to work their appointments into the schedules of these professionals. Your clients will treat you with the same respect as long as you are clear about it yourself.

Didn't you set up a private practice so that you could be your own boss and call the shots?

It's one more way of giving yourself a little love, is it not?

The Essence of Chapter Ten

- Have a few standard phrases and actions to use when you have finished a session, your client is dressed, and you need to move on to the next thing on your agenda.
- Be mindful of your time, being careful to fit in all the necessary work and errands so you have blocks of time that are fully your own for discretionary purposes.
- Notice when your boundaries feel stretched, and create a strategy to protect the time that you need for yourself.

CHAPTER 11: AVOIDING BURNOUT

Burnout could also be called "when you're giving, giving, giving and never receiving." In the field of massage therapy, it is very easy to be the one who is constantly giving to others. Someone says they need something, and hey, we're right there. Something hurts? Here, I know where to press. We are proud of our ability to heal. We love that sigh of ecstasy we get from our clients and friends. We love to be needed.

There are many factors that cause burnout. Working too much, days that are too long, not taking vacations, being alone all the time with the problems of the business . . . after a while, it can get to you. You hate to turn a client away, so you book hours when you planned to be home, or at least off duty. You are your own boss, so you have the freedom to come and go, but you also are conscious of the bills needing to be paid. When you're not working, there's no money. Self-employed people take fewer vacations than employees do. Yes, you have the freedom to work yourself to exhaustion, and no one will stop you.

Boredom is another nail in the burnout coffin. Once you start to get tired of the same old problems and the same routine, you find yourself becoming exhausted more easily. You may become cranky and irritable.

These are common issues that many people in private practices face, so if any of this sounds familiar, don't despair. Understanding the ups and downs of private practice is pivotal in creating a lifestyle that supports you emotionally as well as financially.

Self-Care

You're in the business of showing people how to take care of themselves. Now you need to be your own best friend and do the same for yourself. Massage is very demanding of our physical and emotional energy. We need to replenish that energy so that we can approach each client from a fully restored, energetic place.

Get Massages

You must make sure you get nurturing. How long do you go between receiving massages? A week? Two weeks? A month? More than a month?

I often arranged trades with other massage therapists, as we all do. The ones that worked the best went like this. We met every week at the same time, and either it was my turn or the other person's turn. Like clockwork, every two weeks I was sure to get a massage. It adds to the relaxation that after receiving a massage the recipient doesn't have to give one— they can fully enjoy letting go.

It's also worth patronizing another massage therapist from time to time, spreading the massage prosperity around and receive healing without having to give anything back, except money. These days I am too busy to trade, so that is what I primarily do. There are a couple of people whom I go to regularly, and it feels good to be on the receiving end. I am always so appreciative. It's a treat to get a massage when you don't have to give one back at all. It's the same luxury your clients enjoy—of going in, getting a massage, and being pampered. It's also a great way to learn new techniques.

Take Time Off

It's important to give yourself getaways, both long and short. Being in another environment helps us get different perspectives on our lives. We can recharge and be filled up with new juice and ideas.

My favorite vacations involve getting lost in nature, either in the mountains or out at the ocean. But I know other people who get a great deal of enjoyment by going to a city with a bustling cultural and art community where they get a boost from all the creative stimulation.

Make sure you are taking at least a couple days off each week and spending part of that time doing something fun.

Occasionally take a three-day weekend and go away somewhere. It doesn't take a whole week in the tropics to recharge your batteries. Often just a couple of days out of town can give you a fresh perspective, and you can return feeling rejuvenated. If you don't have money for a vacation and need a getaway, go camping. Visit a friend you haven't seen in a while. Or take a few days off while staying at home and plan a special outing for the day such as spending time at the beach or hiking someplace pretty.   Engage in community events, such as a music festival, an art show, or whatever experience you personally find nurturing that will lift your spirits and give you that "life is good" feeling. You need time away from your routine so that you can appreciate your life. The life of a massage therapist is a good one. You perform a great service. You see appreciative people. You work in a peaceful, relaxed atmosphere. But if you never get away, even the most pleasant of working conditions can become boring and irritating. So you need a change of scenery once in a while.

Fear of Turning Away Work

The reasons self-employed people have a hard time taking vacations is the fear of turning away work.

They are afraid of having time pass without money coming in. They worry that if they go away, business will drop off and they won't be able to get it back.

When I met my husband, a man with a job that included two-week vacations, I had not taken more than four days off at a time in seven years. This was a real wake-up call that made me aware of how I had become a slave to the private practice. Vacations always sounded like a great idea, but I wouldn't give them to myself. I frequently felt jealous of clients who were off to one exotic place or another, and I would listen wistfully as they told me about their adventures. But my fears of being away from my practice kept me from taking myself away from my regular client schedule. My husband made me take vacations. We would go away for a week, just like "normal people." I learned that my world and my business did not end just because I took a break.

Plan for Time Away

Budgeting money, as we have discussed earlier, is critical to the survival of a small business owner. You have to make sure you always have enough. We certainly do that where our bills are concerned. But what about the pleasurable expenses we need?

Set up a special bank account just for time off. Put money into it regularly, and plan your vacations within that budget. Do not charge your vacations on plastic if you can help it. When you start a business, your income will be unstable for a while. You want to keep debts to a minimum. Spend what money you have on a getaway—but only what you have. This is a very important lesson. It is not nurturing yourself to indulge in pleasure while putting yourself in debt at the same time. As I discussed, there are inexpensive ways to recharge without spending a lot of money.

These are a few of the reasons why I didn't take vacations. Do you find yourself having similar concerns? You have to take at least one week off every six months. Seminars and conventions don't count, unless you plan to take additional time off to play. You will not go broke. You will not lose your clients. You will still have your business to come back to. And you will return recharged, with more energy to give to your clients and your work.

Treat Yourself Often

You are pouring your energy out constantly. You are always on, always focused on others. You must get back as much as you are putting out, or where will your energy come from? You can't draw from an empty well.

Indulge in small joyful treats throughout the day. Take yourself out for a really good meal at least once a week. Buy yourself flowers. Get a special scented bath preparation to bathe in. Take a walk in nature as often as you can. Bring a book to the park and enjoy a sunny day outside, relaxing. Do what nurtures you, as much as possible. Make sure there are lots of little pleasures interspersed between massage clients and taking care of business operations. Just for fun, make a list of little things that you can do to recharge throughout the day. Here are a few ideas.

- Take a walk
- Listen to music
- Do some yoga
- Visit a bookstore
- Go the park
- Nap on the massage table
- Meet a friend for dinner
- Arrange a lunch date
- Buy flowers
- Visit nearby shop owners
- Eat lunch in the park
- See a movie
- Dance to some music
- Take a walk in nature
- Journal at a coffee shop

What else can you add? Write down five things you can do to take breaks during the day.

Get Support

A solo practice can get lonely. This is true of any business where you are working alone. As much as it's nice to practice in a quiet, peaceful environment where you are in control, after a while it can feel isolating. This is quite normal. Just about everyone I've talked to tells me that they experience this to some extent. Especially when you work weekends, as many massage therapists do, it can be more difficult to feel socially connected. You are also dealing with the many practical issues that come up when you own a business. Particularly in the early years, you will encounter many problems for the first time. It can make a huge difference to your quality of life if you have people to talk to about these things.

Peer Groups

It helps to have regular connections with other professionals. You can help each other with brainstorming when someone has a problem. There are other people in similar situations who may have dealt with a situation you're grappling with before. Look for groups both in your community and online where you can find like-minded people with whom to connect.

Facebook has a number of groups for exactly this purpose. Do some searches to find a group or two to join. In the search bar at the top of the page type in "Massage", "Massage therapy", or "Massage groups" and see what comes up. Often these groups are closed, but you can still join them. You will see a "join" button, which you can click. The group will have a moderator who makes sure that the people joining the group are appropriate. These groups have lively discussions, and people often pose questions about complicated situations in order to get feedback from the members.

Yahoo groups are another way of connecting with massage therapists via the internet. These groups are email-based, but you can also choose to read all the messages online. Yahoo groups have a better system for organizing files than the Facebook groups. Search for "Yahoo groups," and when the page comes up, there will be a search tool where you can put in the criteria you are looking for.

In addition to online groups, it really helps to meet with people face-to-face. Consider organizing a group of other professionals with whom you could meet regularly, share ideas, and help each other. Contact some other entrepreneurs you know to see about meeting once a week for breakfast or lunch. They don't need to be people in the same field. Solo proprietors have a lot in common, even if their professions differ. If you're getting together often, you will be able to stay abreast of the changes that each person goes through. Monthly meetings work, too, but a lot can happen in a month.

For a while, I met for a weekly breakfast at 7:00 a.m. with a few other business people I knew. It was social, as well as professionally helpful. We were in different fields, but we shared many of the same challenges. We all need people with whom to bounce ideas off of. It's often easier to see a solution for someone else's problem than for our own.

Think about something you could organize easily. A group of 3-5 people is a good size. If you don't know people to invite, start to go to some local events that attract small business owners. If you attend a few of these, eventually you will get to know people you'll like and form deeper relationships.

At one point, I started a small group with a few local health practitioners I knew so we could get to know each other and support one another. I invited an MD, a chiropractor, an eye doctor, a holistic health practitioner, and a hypnotist. We were all in the early years of our practices and eager to meet other people in the community who could be referral sources. We also needed people with whom we could share ideas and trouble shoot problems. This group met for a couple of years and forged some very valuable relationships.

You don't have to know people that well or already be friends with them to do this. If there is someone you like, perhaps someone you have seen for your own health needs at some point, approach them about being part of a group. Many people will welcome this, because they very likely would also like to have some support.

This can lead to wonderful long-term professional relationships as well as personal friendships.

Service Corps of Retired Executives (SCORE)

A great free resource can be found at score.org. This organization is composed of retired business people who want to help mentor others. I called them very early on when I first set up my office and I was totally overwhelmed. You can go to their website and search on your locality, as this is a nationwide organization. There were members even in the small town where I was practicing. These are experienced people who can help you with many business issues.

Professional Support

You may need to shop around until you find the right person, but I highly recommend locating a professional with whom you can work—someone who can answer your questions and give you sound advice. There are going to be situations where you don't want to burden your friends and colleagues, but where you will need help figuring out the right thing to do.

For example, you may be feeling lost about what to do next. Perhaps you had an idea for marketing yourself and it didn't work out the way you thought it would. It is quite natural, in the exploration of trial and error, to sometimes reach a place where you feel stuck and can use some wise, experienced guidance.

Seeing a professional gives you someone with whom to form a strategy and check in with at regular intervals to stay on track. They will give you their undivided attention and will help you find the answers to your problems. Your sessions are confidential. You can safely show them your strengths and weaknesses. They will be able to help you see how to magnify your skills and talents and be at your best. They can also give you an honest assessment as far as how they see your next steps and help you get where you want to go with your business.

I hired consultants at various points in my career and found it extremely worthwhile. Like I have said, there are times when one can feel very alone and overwhelmed. I found people who were both savvy about business and also knew a lot about the holistic health world, and who helped me in ways I never would have imagined on my own. There are times when I felt stuck and I desperately needed to find someone who understood me, and the kind of practice I wanted to create and who knew what I needed to do to get there. Sometimes there was inner work I needed to do in order to make it happen. That is often the case. Creating your own business is a powerful personal growth experience.

The consultants helped me to recognize the role I played in the world, and they showed me how to best present myself to my community. They also gave me their feedback when I was creating materials to hand out to clients. They taught me how to approach other professionals and to network with confidence. They gave me really good suggestions about how to promote myself in my community. And there was one who really helped me get through some of the emotional barriers that were holding me back. She understood and she had great strategies to help me overcome my fears and resistance.

I highly recommend hiring a business consultant when you:

- Are beginning something new
- Feel stuck
- Need input on something you are designing, such as a website or promotional materials
- Have questions about your business

- Have a difficult business problem and need someone objective to talk to
- Would like someone with whom you can check in regularly and evaluate your progress

There are many times when an hour or two of professional help can make all the difference. You may require a lot of help in the beginning, and then, as things evolve, just check in when you want help with something specific.

Seeing a consultant can relieve you of stress, just like getting a massage can. It can greatly take the pressure off and calm your anxiety, knowing that there is someone knowledgeable looking out for you.

Inspiration

There's nothing to bring you back to life when you're feeling depleted like something that inspires you. Seek out people, events, and activities that make you feel happy and help you feel good about your life. These can be absolutely anything that lifts your spirits.

I look for people and events in my community that I find uplifting and restorative. Whether it's going to a bookstore to meet a favorite author and hear them read from their new book, or to a yoga or meditation class, or an art event, I seek out opportunities to be reminded of life's goodness.

I love to dance and I frequently attend a Friday night dance jam, where I can let go of my mental chatter and get lost by moving to the music. I usually go by myself, as a partner is not required. There is a DJ and a room with a beautiful wooden dance floor. No alcohol or food is sold. No particular type of dance is emphasized. It's purely about freedom of movement. Every time I go to one of these, I feel all my earthly cares drift away and my spirits are restored.

Curling up with a good book is another way to get away from it all and get lost in another world.

It's important to make time for these things. You may feel busy and overwhelmed by all the things you have on your plate. It may feel hard to squeeze in an evening or afternoon activity that is something just for fun, just for your enjoyment. But it is so important to do that for yourself. You will come away from these activities with a different perspective—not just about your business, but about your life as a whole.

Do yourself a favor and make this a regular practice.

The Essence of Chapter Eleven

- To avoid burnout, incorporate regular self-care activities into your life.
- Take time off every so often, whether it's a day off at home, a weekend getaway or a lengthy vacation. Make sure you have frequent breaks of some kind.
- Get support by forming groups or activities with peers who can encourage you.

- When you have bigger issues to address, hire a professional consultant or coach to help you iron things out and move forward.
- Seek things out that inspire you and give you a new perspective on life.

This is a famous illustration. What do you see? Depending on how you look at this drawing, you either see a vase or two profiles. You may be wondering what on earth this has to do with your massage business?

The point of the drawing is to demonstrate that we have a choice about how to view any situation. We can either see the goblet or we can see the profiles. They are both there, but sometimes we get so fixated on one that we cannot see the other. It's another way of talking about the glass half empty, glass half full idea.

At this point, you are launched. You've got your practice set up and you have a marketing plan in place to keep new clients coming in. Now, it's merely a matter of getting through the first few years of building up your practice. You will have highs and lows. There will be weeks of delirious delight when the phone is ringing off the hook, you get referrals from clients who love you, and someone buys a gift certificate for everyone in her office. Other weeks will drag with too many unfilled hours in your schedule, and you may start to fret and fall into a spiral of negative thinking.

I am here to tell you that the ebb and flow of a private practice is normal. You will have slow weeks interspersed with busy ones. It takes a few years to really get enough of a clientele going before you can comfortably rely on your business to completely support you. You'll probably need part-time income from another source for a while until you get on your feet. For the first year of my business, I did some freelance sewing for a company that made high-end kites. Every week I took home a pile of cut-out nylon shapes and sewed them together at home. I had control over my hours, so I could be available to drive over to my office whenever I had a client. In the meantime, I had the sewing work to fill in. After a year, the kite company moved to Hawaii and my job went away. However, my massage practice sustained me from that point.

I was lucky that it only took a year. Depending on many factors, such as how much involvement you have in the community, your specialties, how much marketing you do, your visibility, and the current state of the economy, it could take longer. Remember, when I began my business there were hardly any massage therapists working in private practice. Today they're practically on every street corner. But whereas I had to convince people that massage was something to do more often than once a year on their birthday, massage has gone mainstream and many people get bodywork on a regular basis. Your task is to find those people who will especially gravitate to you. It isn't necessary to have everyone want you, just fifteen to twenty people (more or less) per week. Regardless of how many other therapists there are, your unique personality and style will draw clients to you.

Happiness is an Inside Job

Here's how to keep your spirits up. Much of the process of developing a business is extremely creative. Decorating your office, choosing your linens and accoutrements, even figuring out your marketing strategy gets your ideas and imagination flowing, and this feeds your spirit. To a certain extent, these activities will continue, but not as absorbingly as when first setting up. Once you are launched, one thing to be aware of is that you will be spending a lot of time alone during the slower intervals, and there's nothing like unstructured time to get the monkey-mind going. Yes, I've been there, and so have all my massage therapist friends. I want to address this because you have done something remarkable, having taken control of your life and creating your dream. I don't want to see you worry yourself sick just because you have nothing else to do.

Number One – Do Not Compare Yourself to Others.

This is one of the most crazy-making things we can do to ourselves, and it's an easy trap for us to fall into. I hear from one friend that she's swamped at a time when I'm having trouble getting even one client each day. What's wrong with me, I wonder? The answer is nothing. Perhaps my colleague is busy because of a few people she knows who are referring friends to her. Maybe there is an activity she is involved in which is giving her some exposure and spreading the word about what she does. For all I know, her business is slow during times when I am busy, but of course I'm too preoccupied to notice then. There are a million reasons why someone is suddenly busy. Like I have said, it only takes about fifteen or twenty people to fill your schedule, so it's quite conceivable that your friend or colleague just happens to be having a busy week when you're having a slow one.

Number Two - Focus on What's Working.

There is a natural tendency to focus on what's wrong and needs to be fixed. We can do that to the extent that it's all we see. I'll decide my office needs to be re-decorated or there's something important I need to add to the website or I think I have to find some retail products to sell to supplement my services. There's always something that can be improved. Yet if we spend too much of our attention just looking for the things that need to be fixed, we run the risk of always feeling inferior, only seeing the problems. Instead, give yourself credit for your accomplishments. Notice what has improved in your life since last year.

What have you learned that has really made a difference? What new thing are you doing that you absolutely love? What life lessons have you learned that you can now share with your clients? You would not be in this field if you were not someone who is interested in ways to improve themselves and their life.

Likewise, you most likely seek out new things to learn about living a better life because you, by nature are a seeker. Cultivate an awareness of gratitude. Be conscious of the many blessings in your life that you can count.

Number Three – Do Things that Nurture You, as Much as Possible.

How do you recharge? Do you get bodywork or other types of healing? Do you play music? Go out dancing? Do you go for hikes? Ride your bike on country roads? Take a Southeast Asian cooking class? Go camping at a favorite state park? What do you do to refresh your spirit? How often do you do that? I do some of the above things as often as I can. I also make sure I have many small moments of sweetness every day.

I take great pleasure in every meal, no matter how small. I try to make all food special. Even if it's just an apple, I try to make it an apple I got at the farmer's market and I'll eat it with some cheese or nut butter, all laid out on a beautiful ceramic plate—turning a simple fruit break into a fancy hors d'oeuvre. I try to get some exercise every day. Often it's in the form of a walk someplace pretty, even just a nearby street where the houses have lush gardens. And if the weather's not good for walking, I'll put on music and dance. It makes me happy. I cannot fully express the importance of doing things daily that make you happy. Everything else will fall into place. Your practice will fill up. People will love you and refer others to you. Your bank account will grow strong.

You will have ups and downs, busy times and slow times. This is the reality for everyone who has ever been self-employed. Keeping up your spirits by constantly nurturing yourself is an essential health practice. And I promise you, once you realize how vital this is, you will be encouraging your clients to do the same.

Number Four - Stay Inspired

It's important to have things in your life that keep you going emotionally, spiritually and creatively. We all have our moments of doubt when we can use some positive reminders to take care of ourselves. It's helpful to have stories that others share to make us feel less isolated and more understood.

I wrote this book to inspire and encourage massage therapists and help them launch their businesses. I have known so many fabulous massage therapists that had a hard time putting themselves out there in the business world. This is often the case with sensitive, intuitive people.

All my life I have enjoyed writing. Since my days in high school, writing the poetry of a teenager's tortured soul, and through much of my life, writing has been something that grounds me. It's part of my passion. So I combined these things. I decided to write about what I've learned through the journey of creating a massage business in the hopes that my stories and experiences would help others feel empowered to take those bold steps. For those who already had businesses, I hoped to give them new ideas and encouragement. Reading inspiring books is so incredibly helpful when you have a business. It certainly was for me.

The things that inspire me are the nourishment that feeds my dreams. I recently read Elizabeth Gilbert's book, "Big Magic," which is about following your creative energy. Stephen Pressfield's book, "The War of Art" is another book about the creative process that kept me going while I wrote this book. The writer Anne Lamott is another one of my mentors, as she very humorously helps us laugh at our faults as we face our challenges. Her deeper message is how life is a spiritual journey with a very irregular and twisted road.

I am fascinated by books, particularly memoirs, because I love reading the true stories of how people get through tough challenges. This is what I do in my spare time, when I feel the need for a boost. I read. I watch movies that either have an important message or make me laugh. I listen to music. We need our sources of inspiration to keep us going. What do you do when you need to be uplifted?

Number Five - Follow Your Heart

Trust your gut. That is what led you to this field in the first place. Something about bodywork really captured your heart. It felt right. You were moved. Perhaps you received a session at a critical time in your life, and that made you want to learn that kind of healing. Following your heart has led you to create your very own massage practice. Don't stop. What's next?

What fascinates you? What more do you want to learn? What else do you want to experience? What are you drawn to? Remember, don't feel the need to do what another bodyworker is doing, merely because it seems like the thing to do. Just because someone you know is now selling relaxing music, or teaching a yoga class, or incorporating nutritional counseling into their practice, don't think you have to do this too, unless it really rocks your world. People become successful because of the things they are passionate about. Their clients sense the excitement and conviction they have about the things they find interesting, and that's what attracts them. This will work for you, too. Do what really means something to you and others will find you magnetic. Let it come from your heart, from what really turns you on.

Remember, you are a role model for your clients. They not only see you as someone who can loosen up their tight muscles, but as an example of healthy living. As I said earlier, they will project all kinds of things onto you, partly because they want to see you that way. For instance, many of my clients assumed I was a vegetarian. I'm not. They also assumed I did a lot of spiritual practice. I do. They viewed me as someone who could guide them, not just physically, but spiritually and emotionally into a happier place. Therefore, all the work I was doing on myself was something I could share with them. Not necessarily my problems, but the tools I was using to work through them.

As you can see by everything in this book, having a successful massage practice is much more than knowing the right pressure points and physical skills. It's more than savvy marketing. It's a culmination of everything that you are. It's having the courage to share those things that have deep meaning for you and that make you one of a kind.

The work of a massage therapist becomes a lifestyle. Since you are drawn towards nurturing modalities, there is a flow between what you do during your personal time to learn about healthy practices and what you are able to share with your clients. You will always be aware of your position as an example. It encourages you to be your best self.

Savor the fruits of your labor. You spent your whole life to get where you are now. Let your heart and intuition be your guide. Trust your gut. Live your dream. Enjoy this wonderful life you have created for yourself!

The Essence of Chapter Twelve

- Have a toolbox of things you love that inspire you and keep your spirits up.

- Give yourself credit for your accomplishments.
- Explore new things that you can add to your repertoire.
- Appreciate the good life you have created.
- Practice gratitude.

CHAPTER 13: CONVERSATION WITH ED LARK, MASSAGE THERAPIST AND INSTRUCTOR

Ed Lark has been practicing and teaching massage therapy since the 90s. He lives in Sebastopol, California, where he has a large and loyal client base specializing in neuromuscular therapy. In addition, he works closely with medical and complementary health care providers in team approaches as a therapeutic massage specialist for the treatment of acute and chronic pain.

Ed has taught at several institutions, including the National Holistic Institute in Emeryville, California; the Massage Therapy Institute in Davis, California; the Western Institute of Science and Health in Rohnert Park, California; and the Harbin School of Healing Arts in Middletown, California. He also teaches massage and deep tissue intensives in France.

I sat down with Ed to talk about the massage field and get his thoughts about what he thinks people beginning a career in bodywork ought to know.

Molly: Briefly tell me what got you into massage.

Ed: I had been in my circle of friends for about ten years— the guy that people would sit in front of at parties, 'cause I'd work on their neck and shoulders. People would lie down on the floor, I'd work on their backs. I was an electrician. I didn't really know anything about the body or about massage. I had never had a massage. But I would work on peoples' neck and shoulders. My hands knew where to go. So, it was strongly suggested by one person I was working on...she had asked me what school I went to...and I said, "I don't know. I'm just an electrician. I just do this." So she suggested that I go to school to learn massage. And looking back, it was the best advice I'd ever received. So I started going to massage school. And two months— actually, less than that—probably two weeks into my year-long training. I knew that this was what I'd be doing the rest of my life.

Molly: Cool. You loved it.

Ed: I loved it so much. It just felt right. And six months into my year-long training I found a job that allowed me to leave my electrician job and go into massage full-time and I've been doing it ever since.

Molly: What was that?

Ed: Selling massage tables at a small store and doing chair massages in the store as well.

Molly: Ahhh, was that your first massage job?

Ed: Yes, that was my first foot into the industry, and that was the beginning of many things that I did for a living during my first years. It was all in the massage trade. I decided that everything I'd be doing from now on would be somehow in the trade.

Molly: Somehow related to massage.

Ed: Yes. It was a good thing. I worked a lot.

Molly: So how did you start building a practice?

Ed: Well, it initially started with friends. I needed people to practice on during massage school. I began showing people what I could do, and that started getting me word of mouth clients. I worked for a chiropractor in Oakland, and through that, I started getting more clinical massage clients, people with more therapeutic needs, which is the line that I went towards because I like the more clinical work. A lot of the clients who came through the chiropractor became clients of mine and then word of mouth just spreads. You know, that sort of thing. I worked at UC Berkeley for a few years. When I first graduated I got a job at UC Berkeley.

Molly: Doing what?

Ed: Massage.

Molly: Where? How did you do it at the school?

Ed: At the UC Berkeley Rec Center. They have a whole fitness center.

Molly: Oh really? And they had a massage room?

Ed: Yeah. They had a massage program.

Molly: Wow! For the students!

Ed: For anybody.

Molly: Wow. I didn't know that.

Ed: Anybody who uses the gym. They can be from the public, faculty, students, or staff at the university. And they all have massage available to them at a fairly good rate.

Molly: I had no idea.

Ed: So I was doing five clients a day, three days a week for them, as a way of just practicing, getting my hands on as many people as I could and it was a fair base income while I built my practice. So I was balancing UC Berkeley, the chiropractor and my private practice, which was slow in the beginning, of course, but slowly building. And then on weekends I would do chair massage at conventions and trade shows through a company in San Francisco. I did that for a few years. For a while I worked seven days a week.

Molly: Wow. That's a lot of work!

Ed: I did anything I could do to get my hands on people. And it paid off. Then as one thing becomes more and more lucrative, you start weeding out the lesser paying jobs. You know, you just stick with what's working best.

Molly: Like you're starting to do now—letting go of ILM *(Ed has been doing massage for the staff at the famous special effects company, Industrial Light and Magic)*

Ed: Yes. Absolutely. I'm getting everything I need from my private practice now.

Molly: So what advice do you have for someone starting out?

Ed: Just focus on the quality of your touch. That's what people are ultimately going to come back for. To be authentic in themselves and really focus on the quality and give clients the best work you can.

Molly: Mmm hmmm.

Ed: Don't focus on the money. Focus on the excellence in whatever it is you do. That's what's going to make your work stand out from everyone else's.

Molly: You were talking earlier about service.

Ed: Yes, understanding that massage therapy is a service industry is very, very important. We do it because we love to do it. We love to help people. And like I said earlier, we don't do it just for the money. The money is a wonderful side effect. But you really have to have a desire to serve. To really help people, no matter who lies on your table. To be non-judging, to be totally present to whatever falls on your table and to be truly there for them. When someone's on your table, that's the most important thing. In your world, in that moment is the person on your table and giving them the best experience you can.

Molly: If you were starting your career right now, is there anything you would do differently?

Ed: Oh...that's an interesting question.

Molly: With the perspective you have now?

Ed: If I were starting massage?

Molly: Yes, if you were starting your massage career now. I mean, it's a different world now.

Ed: It is a different world now. I don't know if I would really do anything differently. I think I would just get my hands on people as much as I could. Whatever I focus on, I try to put 100% into it. I would just continue to learn. I mean I'm a big believer that the more you know your tools, the anatomy, and the physiology, the more that enhances your intuition. I embraced that right from the very beginning. I don't think I'd do anything differently.

Molly: How did you get into teaching?

Ed: I started at UC Berkeley. They asked me to do classes for the staff on self-care, and so I'd go into their different departments, the workers, the secretaries, the staff—all those people—I would show them how to work on their hands and wrists, how to do stretching to counteract the computer use. Then, during finals, I would go up to the dorms and teach the students how to give each other neck and shoulder massages during those stressful times.

Molly: So that was your first time teaching people...

Ed: ...to massage each other. Exactly. And then they had me do little Intro to Massage classes for anyone. Sometimes there'd be only five or six people. I would show them how they could work on each other informally, just on a blanket on the floor. I would have small classes at the rec center, too, on how to do basic massage.

Molly: So you've been teaching almost from the beginning.

Ed: Yes. And then two years after I graduated I was invited to teach at National Holistic Institute by my teachers. My career counselor became a really good friend and she suggested that I go and become a teacher. I found that teaching has done nothing but reinforce my practice. It's kept me current and kept me up on anatomy. Teaching has always reinforced my private practice.

Molly: What do you think that students need to know? Any advice for them as far as marketing?

Ed: Well, embracing and welcoming the slow times. Because there's always going to be slow times. And knowing that persevering through the slow times is a huge thing.

Molly: What should they do during slow times?

Ed: Take care of themselves. Not to punish themselves by wallowing in it, but celebrate who they are. If they like hiking, go for hikes. Don't let it get them down. Follow up on leads, of course, bringing cards with them, handing out cards, making connections, but not lose track of who they are. Slow times can bring people down energetically.

Molly: How do you maintain your boundaries? As far as time...?

Ed: <laughs> You may be asking the wrong person.

Molly: It's an issue that I see happen a lot with massage therapists, which is why I have suggested schedules. People have a tendency to feel like they should be available whenever anyone might want them, so they get kind of strung out.

Ed: Yes, knowing your boundaries with timing is important. Now I work five days a week. In the beginning, I worked seven days a week. My mistakes about boundaries in the beginning were exactly that. I didn't turn anything down. But knowing how to say "no" is important. I didn't know that in the beginning.

Molly: People are afraid to ever turn somebody away.

Ed: I pushed myself seven days a week—trade shows on the weekends, chiropractor would be one half of the day, other half of the day would be UC Berkeley. And then trying to fit in private clients in all the spaces in between. I ran myself ragged for almost two years without any breaks and I actually reached a place of burnout.

Molly: Of course! That's gonna happen!

Ed: And what's interesting with burnout, is that you don't even see it coming. I know that's true for me and I see this with other people, too. My energy would weaken, and then I would notice that my client load would start to slow down. It was as though the Universe knew somehow that I was running out of energy. And I was seeing fewer and fewer clients. My slow times were getting really long and I was getting worried.

Molly: When you were burned out?

Ed: Yes. And that happened before I realized how burned out I was.

Molly: So you didn't have the energy for many clients because you were getting burned out and not many people were coming in.

Ed: Exactly. My career counselor asked me when I had my last break and she was surprised when I couldn't remember. So I started letting things go and taking better care of myself. As I started taking better care of myself, magically, I started getting more clients.

Molly: That's a very important point. I've been there myself and I've seen so many massage therapists that have that issue, where they're afraid to turn any work away and as a result they never have real days off. Sometimes they'll have someone at 11:00 in the morning and another person at 4:00 and so they're strung out the whole day because of those two people. When I met my husband, I had not taken more than three days off at a time in eight years. I was afraid to go away. I was afraid my practice would disappear. Then I marry someone who has regular two-week vacations who wants to really go somewhere and it felt scary! Because, of course, he insisted I take at least a week off here and there and I had never stopped working for that long once I had begun my practice.

Ed: I think that's a huge thing. So now I put aside my weekends. Those two days I consider sacred time. Basically, that's time that I'm not going to work, and my clients appreciate it. I think the fear is that if you turn someone away, they're going to go to someone else and they won't be your client anymore or you'll lose money. But ultimately, in turning people away, your clients learn to respect you.

Molly: Exactly.

Ed: Because you're taking care of yourself. They love it when I'm going on vacation. They love it when I take time off. Because they know how hard I work.

Molly: And you're a role model for good self-care.

Ed: And if clients have to wait two weeks for me and they're in need, I can refer them to a friend. They love that. And they still come back.

Molly: That's a very good point.

Ed: So now, I've got a five week trip to Iceland coming up this year and my clients have learned to patiently wait for me. I give them referral numbers while I'm gone, but when I come back, I have a full week or two or three waiting for me.

Molly: Right.

Ed: And at this point, I'm grateful for a very loyal clientele. They love that I take care of myself so that I can then take care of them.

Molly: Yes. This is very important. Because there's two sides to that coin. There's the fear of not getting enough work which keeps people overworking themselves, but the reality is that if they're taking care of themselves they end up with a practice full of loyal clients who respect them. It enables them to have a healthy balance between work and self-care.

Ed: That's exactly right. And that's the way I run my practice now.

Molly: Thank you, Ed. This has been very valuable.

As you can see, Ed's approach is different from mine. Whereas I tend to map out strategies to approach people through the mail, through e-newsletters, and social media, Ed tends to be more social. He makes his connections at social gatherings and through a network of influential people who are in his circles. His style of massaging people everywhere he goes suits his personality. It's who he is and that's how he has become known in his community. From his story, you can see how he jumped at the opportunities to teach early on in his career, and that played a big role in shaping his approach to massage.

The reason I interviewed Ed is because he has a very different story from mine, yet we are both successful. This illustrates how important it is to be true to your own style and personality. The trait we both share is that we love doing massage and are committed to working very hard at it, learning everything we can, and doing whatever it took to build a successful clientele. Ed is unlikely to write a book. Whereas I have always enjoyed writing projects, Ed is an outstanding photographer. He spends his free time backpacking and taking extraordinary photographs of nature. We all are different and we all have our gifts. As do you!

Chapter 14: A Conversation with Ona Goodrich, MT and Acupuncturist

Ona Goodrich practices both massage and acupuncture. She became a massage therapist in the late '90s, and after ten years, she went to acupuncture school to learn new skills and expand her services. Her practice is in a small city of 60,000 people where she has made herself known and has a thriving practice. She has developed her clientele through making many personal connections, and most of her clients come in regularly, allowing her business solid growth.

Her office is located in the center of town in a beautiful old Victorian office building that is home to a large number of private practices, salons, and small businesses.

Molly: Can you say a little bit about how you got started and built up your clientele? This is my readers' number one question!

Ona: When I first started my massage practice, I was so freaked out, wondering how I was going to make it. I thought I had to do many things that felt unnatural to me. Like having a business plan, for example. That's probably a good idea, but that's not who I am. I've never had one and I still don't. There are many things I've thought I should do but didn't because it just wasn't me. It didn't feel right. And it felt fake.

As soon as you feel that you're trying to do something that isn't really you, just stop. It's okay. It'll all work out.

Molly: So what did work?

Ona: I met someone while working at a spa, who also had an office here in town, and she started sending me her overflow. That was the beginning.

Molly: What else did you do?

Ona: I also gave a lot of people who worked in places near me free massages to introduce them to what I was doing. That worked very well. I would do that again.

Molly: Was there any criteria for whom you were offering free sessions?

Ona: Yes, people who were in a position to refer to me if they liked my work. I went to a number of salons, for instance. In fact, in this building I went and talked to everybody and said who I was. And if I thought they might refer clients to me, I offered them a free massage. And then I began reaching out to more people in the community.

For instance, I belonged to 24-Hour Fitness, and they said I could set up a massage chair. I gave 10-minute massages and I did get several clients that way. It also kept me busy. I think it's very important to spend time working in your office, even if you're not making money.

Molly: So giving free massages to people who could experience your work, know its value, and then recommend you to others gave you a chance to be in your office working and kept you busy.

Ona: Yes, just talking to people here in the building enabled me to get known pretty quickly, even though it was just a few people in the beginning. There was a psychotherapist who started coming in regularly. There is a medical doctor who has been coming in for years. It's slow, but it's very worthwhile. My practice grew through a lot of word of mouth.

Molly: I think that being in a building like this with a lot of other professionals gave you a great opportunity to meet people in a low key, casual way that helped you get known. I want to give my readers a lot of different approaches to getting their practices started.

Ona: Well, one thing I wouldn't do, which is something that's become very popular, is advertising with Groupon and other services where people are giving away their work for almost nothing.

Molly: I agree. I think it cheapens the work.

Ona: It cheapens everything connected with it. I have a bad taste in my mouth about that. Honestly, I would rather offer a complimentary massage to someone with whom I have a connection than to promote my services at a cut rate to strangers.

Molly: So, in the beginning, you were getting the overflow from the other massage therapist in this building and giving free sessions to people you met who would spread the word and send you referrals. Then what happened?

Ona: The person who sent me her overflow eventually moved. But not many of her clients came to me. People don't shift to another person that easily. That's one piece of advice I have. Never buy another person's practice. People do not automatically go to someone else when their therapist retires or leaves town. If someone they know refers them to a therapist they like, that's one thing. But if a therapist says they're leaving and another person is taking over, their clients don't automatically go to the new person. I even told her that I would honor her unredeemed gift certificates. But I don't even think five or ten people came in from those.

Molly: Interesting. That's good advice.

Ona: In the beginning, I found it was very important to stay busy. Even if I was doing it for free, I was letting new people experience my work. It was really critical for me to have clients to massage and not worry whether this was going to fly. As long as I could keep busy giving massages, I felt okay.

Molly: So offering free massages to the appropriate people was a good way to get started, because that way you're busy working rather than worrying.

Ona: Yes, and you're in your space. I think being in your office, doing good work, filling it with your positive energy is important.

Molly: What other words of advice do you have for new therapists?

Ona: The most important thing is knowing you're making a long-term commitment, taking your time with it, and steadily building it up. Not expecting success overnight, but if you know in your heart it's what you want to do, just keep putting it out there to people.

You know, it wasn't a big dream of mine to be a massage therapist. I thought it was something I was just going to do for a short while. So I didn't have a big vision of what it was going to be. I think that's important to realize. A lot of people don't start out knowing exactly how they want their practice to unfold.

Molly: I think that's true of many people. I know that was true of me. I just did it while I was going to college studying psychology. It was how I was putting myself through school. But by the time I was done with college I had a massage practice full of clients and it evolved from there. I didn't plan it like this.

Ona: Yes, me too. And I think that someone who comes at it from a more medical or scientific approach will have a different kind of bodywork practice.

Molly: Most of the people I know just fell into it. They enjoyed doing massage and thought it would be part-time supplementing something else and then things evolved into their primary livelihood.

Ona: It's very rewarding work. One of the things I love is people thanking you. People are happy to see their massage therapist.

Molly: Yup. People always leave feeling better than when they came in.

Ona: Exactly. And they say, "Thank you so much." That is such a rewarding part of my day! No matter how tired I am. No matter what other things I may be struggling with. People are happy here. And not everybody gets that in their job. Most of the people who come here tell me how much they hate their jobs. And then they tell me, "Oh, you're so good at this! I feel wonderful now!" Who doesn't want to hear that?

Molly: I think it's totally okay to start wherever you are and let it evolve. Get support and learn what need to as it grows. Because, as you say, there are so many things that aren't going to make sense until you're doing them.

Ona: Yes. I feel like I'm just finally starting to get organized.

Molly: Five years into being an acupuncturist?

Ona: Yes. There were things I never felt like doing before, like having a good bookkeeping program.

Molly: Do you use a bookkeeping program now?

Ona: Oh, I sure do. But I didn't until I became an acupuncturist. I wish I had known more about business when I started. Like, knowing what accounts receivable is. That kind of thing. When you learn about it in school, it doesn't make as much sense as when you're actually doing it. I would advise people to wait to take business classes until they're actually in practice. During the first year or two when they're not so busy with clients, they have time to create a foundation for their business.

That's the time to join a massage Facebook group. Or a small business Facebook group. I'm in a small business group that I really like. And it's a small enough that I feel really connected to those people.

Molly: What about in-person groups?

Ona: The problem with that is scheduling. That's what I like about Facebook groups. You don't have to all pull out your calendars and then have to deal with a conflict when one person can't make a meeting and they want the whole group to reschedule.

Molly: Do you ever feel like an online group is a bit impersonal?

Ona: Not if it's small enough. I like the size of the Facebook business group I'm in. There are about 40 members. I haven't met all of them, but there are several that live within an hour from here so I certainly could.

Molly: That's a good size, where you can all get to know each other. It helps where you can really talk about the issues that come up in having a business. They don't have to be in the same field as you.

Ona: Oh, not at all. As long as what they're doing is similar enough, you can share what you're going through and help each other. That way you don't have to feel isolated even though you have a solo practice. Otherwise it can be overwhelming. Even fifteen years into doing massage I value this.

Molly: What was it that inspired you to go into acupuncture?

Ona: I needed to take care of my body. I know I'm going to have to work forever. Some people can do massage full-time forever. I'm not sure I can. And I like having the balance. I don't think I'd want to do either one full-time. I wouldn't want to do only acupuncture. People are not as happy after acupuncture as they are after massage. They're grateful for the help, but their eyes don't light up in the same way. Massage is really wonderful!

Molly: Do you have a lot of clients who do both with you?

Ona: Sometimes, but for the most part I have different people that come for each modality. Most of my massage clients are very regular. I do get new people who float in and out, but mostly regulars.

Molly: That's wonderful.

Ona: And then somebody will move away and I still get panicked about losing that regular income, but a new person always fills in. It's interesting that I still have that anxiety after all this time and I have to remind myself that it's going to be okay. It always ends up okay. Whatever your fears are, being in business can amplify them, especially in the beginning. It's a good opportunity to learn about yourself.

Molly: Absolutely. I have always said that having your own business is the greatest personal growth experience because all of your stuff comes up. All of your fears, all of your neuroses, because you're relying on yourself for your survival. That's why I went to a lot of workshops, especially in the beginning. I found it was important to have positive ways to work with your issues. That's where the practices of self-care come in.

Ona: I think workshops and spiritual practices are definitely self-care. Having rituals that support you are self-care, such as doing a brief meditation or pulling an angel card or some type of daily inspiration. Rituals help. They create foundation. They help you stay grounded. Because when you start a business you have to create EVERYTHING. You decide color of the room. Everything about the room. It's all your own creation. And if you've always been an employee, you don't realize how much has been provided for you. The leap from working in a spa to creating my own business was a huge deal. I had so many decisions to make. What kind of sheets should I have? Even that seemed overwhelming in the beginning. What should it look like? What music should I have? That used to drive me crazy. (laughs)

Molly: It's a lot of little decisions. But it's also very creative.

Ona: Yes it is, and I still enjoy that part.

Molly: It's a journey. For some people, their journey is about their relationships, their marriages, or having children. And for others the big journey is all the things they learn in creating a business—having something meaningful they do and figuring out how to plug it into the world. We have different focuses at different times in our lives.

Ona: Yes, and it can all be viewed as part of a spiritual practice.

Molly: Looking back, when you were starting out, is there anything you would have done differently?

Ona: I don't think at the time that I was brave enough, but I would have worked less. By that, I mean I would have had better boundaries about my hours so I wasn't always available. I would have charged more and worked less. I'm still working on that to a certain degree.

Molly: What's hard about that?

Ona: Probably having a strong enough sense of self-value and confidence. The hardest part for me isn't with new people. It's telling my regular clients that I'm raising my prices. There are times when one has to do that and I love my clients. It's hard to tell them. Tightening up my hours has been easier.

Molly: What else can you add?

Ona: It's very important to be authentic with whatever you do. Like marketing, for example. There are many marketing practices I'm not comfortable doing, but I recently put my name on a bicycle kit someone I know is distributing. I'm a long-time cyclist and I'd like to attract more cyclists. I understand their bodies and I know what they need. So advertising on cycling clothes is actually a pretty good marketing move for me.

Molly: What is it exactly?

Ona: A friend of mine makes steel bikes. And as a way to market his bikes, he has a kit that he sells that has advertising on it. The cycling clothes are called "kits." There's shorts and a jersey and arm warmers and leg warmers for the winter. And they're all called kit. Even cycling shoes are part of their kit. The whole ensemble.

Molly: And your name is on these kits?

Ona: Yes, my name is on the shirts, up at the top. It's really nice.

Molly: Do you pay for that?

Ona: Yes, it's a one time fee of $250.

Molly: I see. You're like a sponsor.

Ona: Yes, exactly. I'm helping to sponsor his cycles.

Molly: That's a smart way to attract cyclists as clients. What do you have them print?

Ona: Just my name: Ona Acupuncture. I have an unusual name so if you Google it, you'll find me.

Molly: Is there anything else you'd like to share?

Ona: I find doing continuing education is important. I hadn't done any in a while and I recently went to Esalen and did a week-long workshop.

Molly: That sounds wonderful.

Ona: It was. That's part of self-care, too.

Molly: What was the thing that you got the most out of that?

Ona: Honestly? Connecting with other people. There were some very good techniques I learned, too. But it was so uplifting to meet other people and hear their stories.

I found it interesting that we learned a lot of techniques on the hips and the legs. And then the following week, a client came in who had just been in a bike crash and he needed exactly what I had learned. So I had the chance to practice right away.

Molly: Awesome! Continuing education is very important.

Ona: Yes, at least every few years.

Molly: I think most states require it. But there's a big value to doing them in person rather than online. There are a lot of places that offer online CEUs.

Ona: Yes, I agree, it is so good to do in person. For instance, I'm not that comfortable doing movement and dance, and every day in the class we did some. It was really good for me. The class pushed me in many ways and I learned a lot. It's good to connect with other people in the field. With my busy schedule, I don't have much time for that on a regular basis, so the continuing education classes are a perfect opportunity. It helps to hear other peoples' stories and get new ideas.

Molly: Agreed. Thank you, Ona. This has been fun!

Ona: For me, too! I've enjoyed having this talk.

A note from Molly: My biggest take away from this interview with Ona is how important it is to find a way to promote yourself that feels natural and comfortable as well as being effective. As she said, Ona is not comfortable with many forms of promotion.

Honestly, marketing is really just a way of getting the word out, however you manage to do it. Whether it's through an ad, social media, direct mail, or personal connections, you have to find a way to do this that suits your personality. For Ona, that was being in an office building right in the center of town, where she could casually and informally connect with a large number of neighboring entrepreneurs. Since many of these businesses were people in the healing arts and personal care industries, they were in a perfect position to refer clients to her. This happened so organically and naturally that it didn't feel like marketing to Ona.

This also shows the importance of choosing the right location for your practice. Being in a place where it was easy to meet other sole proprietors made it easy for Ona to spread the word in a way that felt authentic.

Chapter 15: A Conversation with Roberta Ryan, Business Coach

Roberta is a business coach and the owner of Ryan Business Design. She specializes in guiding business owners who are passionate about making the world a better place. She affectionately refers to them as visionaries, healers, and do-gooders.

Her specialty involves a Discovery Program where, over a course of six sessions, she helps her clients uncover the issues that have eluded them, and then coaches them to design a realistic plan that overcomes those limitations and increases their income and impact in ways that are natural for them. Her work is a combination of intuition and practicality.

Molly: Why don't you begin by telling me a little bit about your business, what you do and the kinds of people that you work with?

Roberta: My clients are solopreneurs—individuals who have found work they really love but have not yet achieved the income or impact they know is possible. They tend to be non-linear thinkers and because of that, parts of business can be challenging for them. I interpret the nuances of business so they can earn more money, increase their impact, and have less stress.

My journey began many years ago when I noticed that two businesses doing the same work in the same community could have vastly different levels of success. I became really curious about why that situation existed, and set off to find the answer. At the same time, I realized that if I could help healers be more successful, the world would be a better place. I work with a lot of coaches, artisans, health care professionals, educators, and health practitioners—all who are healers at heart.

Molly: Do you find that there is a common barrier that keeps people from moving forward with their businesses?

Roberta: Most often, it is lack of skill and experience running a small business. Mixed into that can also be feelings that being in business is a "not quite right thing" to be doing, and they hope that they can just be a practitioner and all those other messy things will take care of themselves.

Molly: How do you address those issues?

Roberta: I talk with them about their beliefs and we find ways for them to reframe their perspective. I also am diligent at coaching them on basic business principles so they can create what they want and still be in alignment with their values.

Molly: Do your clients tend to be new or established businesses?

Roberta: The majority of my clients are established, having been in business at least two years.   It's very different to work with someone who's brand new rather than established.

Molly: Why is this?

Roberta: When someone is a couple years into their work, they have experience of what works and doesn't work for them. They may have taken some business programs but they are not able to make it go where they want it to go. They know, in their guts that it could be better, but are unsure how to change their situation.

When someone is brand new, especially if they have never been self-employed, the help they need is more fundamental.

Molly: I think many people often think it's going to be easier than it turns out to be. One advantage I see in hiring someone like you is that there can be a feeling of being very alone that can be kind of enveloping. They're doing everything by themselves. Problems come up and they have no one to talk to about them. They have hours that are not booked when they wonder what they should be doing. So it's nice to have an actual person whom they're meeting with who can support them, help them, and troubleshoot with them.

Roberta: Molly, you expressed that really well and I agree with you: isolation is a big issue. Hiring a professional is one way to have on-going support, but other options include taking business programs or joining a professional organization.

Molly: What other issues get in the way?

Roberta: As I mentioned above, one universal challenge is that many people do want to think of themselves as "in business." When they begin to see that issue differently, they realize there is a lot they can do to change their situation. As they learn and experiment, everything is less mysterious.

Molly: What's an example of one of these principles?

Roberta: One thing that can help when figuring out how to market is understanding how an individual's mind works when they are making a buying decision. A good way to get a sense of this is to pay attention to the factors that influence how you buy things, especially services similar to your own.

For example, what I noticed is there are three things that influence my choices:

1. Clarity—I want to understand what is offered and the value to me.

2. Visibility—I need to be aware it exists.

3. Credibility—I need to know I can trust the individual to provide what they are promising.

Molly: So it's up to the practitioner to be clear when they put their message out there, every time they're communicating, who they serve and how.

Roberta: Absolutely. It is important to let potential clients know what they do and how they will benefit from their work. A great way to communicate your value is by telling stories about how clients have benefited from your work. For example, a bodyworker might say, "Recently a women came to me who suffered from chronic headaches and had trouble sleeping. She tried a lot of different things and was feeling pretty frustrated. After a couple of sessions, she was pain-free and sleeping soundly, plus she has some new methods she can use herself when she feels the headache coming on. "

Molly: Yes, I see that.

Roberta: Visibility refers to repeatedly putting your message out there whether you are running ads, using social media, or networking. If you think about how we buy something, it's often because we see it presented to us over and over again, and we know where to find it when we need it. For instance, knowing about the woman who is so good at relieving headaches. Someone might be thinking about her and remember that they kept her card when they want to give her work a try because now they need it. It's a matter of consistently being out there.

Molly: Yes, that presents a great and easy opportunity.

Roberta: And the third thing is credibility. You know, there are people that we meet whom we just don't feel good about. For instance, there was someone in a business group I was in who was always late. She never showed up on time. I like her personally and I have heard good things about her work, but her tardiness reduced my confidence in her. I wondered if I were to go and see her if I would end up waiting twenty minutes for her to show up. Something about that behavior made me not want to give her a chance. Or people who don't follow up on their word. There are a lot of ways that we build credibility and it makes a difference when people decide to hire us.

Another example is if a client comes into someone's messy office, that's going to make a negative impression on them, but they might not even realize that's what it is. They may wonder if the person is disorganized and is really incompetent.

Even a simple thing like the timing of the session can affect how clients feel about you. If a person's appointment is scheduled for an hour and the practitioner spends an hour and fifteen minutes, the practitioner isn't being mindful of boundaries. They may think they are giving better service without being aware that they may be making their client late for the next thing they are going to do.

Molly: This is a great topic, because one of the issues I discuss in my book is the importance of setting boundaries. A lot of people I have known in the healing arts have a difficult time sticking to boundaries, particularly time boundaries. They may know what those boundaries are or what they want them to be but they are so motivated to help people that they will ignore the boundary. For instance, if it's more than the time they have allotted or someone needs them on a day they don't work or beyond their normal work hours. If someone needs them, they get so pulled into it, that they often overstep their own boundaries and that accumulates to create a detrimental experience. They get exhausted. They get burned out.

Roberta: Yes, I agree completely. They also may not ask for what they need in terms of payment, and then they find themselves short financially. This can happen on so many levels.

Molly: That's why I think that it's important to explain that business is a lot more than marketing.

Roberta: You are absolutely right. It's everything. It's what the business looks like on the outside and inside, how the practitioner responds to inquiry calls in addition to the quality of service.   When I come in as a consultant to evaluate someone's business, those are the kinds of things that I notice.

I worked with someone who was brand new in business, and at first she would often miss our appointments. She had ADHD, which is not that uncommon with highly creative people. And so, one of the things we worked on in the beginning was finding a way for her to work with her calendar so she could be on time. She and I both knew if she was missing appointments with me, she would also do this with her clients. We had to find a system that was workable for her. For instance, when she began, she was scheduling her clients over five days and she wove her other commitments into the times between her appointments. Her schedule became too complicated. Once we narrowed her work hours down to just Tuesday and Thursday afternoons she found it effortless to keep her business appointments. It's different for everybody, but this is one example of how I worked with someone to develop more credibility.

Molly: Do you encounter people who overextend themselves because they're afraid that if they don't they'll lose clients?

Roberta: That's a very common dynamic. Sometimes it's not so much that they're afraid as that they're so excited to do the work that they don't even care about the extra time they are spending. They'll give way beyond what's healthy for them.

Molly: Yes, I have observed discussions in Facebook groups with people who are excited about their work and want to engage with as many people as possible, but then they start to get exhausted. How do you counsel people about this?

Roberta: I observe the whole business to see how this dynamic affects other factors of their lives. From the framework of balance, when you're overextended it creates depletion on many levels. It can be common with highly creative, intuitive healers. How they approach life becomes part of the whole dialogue, along with pricing. They begin recognizing when they are giving too much and we work to develop a strategy for working with it. For example, I have a client who is an intuitive healer. She runs into clients or people she knows in public and they stop and ask her questions. She gets pulled in and spends a lot of time helping them, but afterwards she feels resentful. So we worked on strategies and ways for her to kindly and politely disengage. We came up with scripts for to use the next time this happens. For instance, she will say to them, "We really need to get together for a one on one session to talk about this." And that stops them from taking advantage of her when they just happen to run into each other in their small community.

Molly: Aha, that's the answer. A script! So when someone who doesn't work on Sundays gets a call from someone who says she's really aching in her shoulders and that Sunday is the only day they're able to come in she needs a script so she has something she can say. The practitioner will have an internal conflict because they really want to help...

Roberta: Especially if it's a good client

Molly: And maybe Sunday is the only time the practitioner has all week to relax. That's a very common conflict. This is where the script comes in. They need a standard response. "I'd love to help you. The soonest I can fit you in is..."

Roberta: Scripts are very important for a great many things. For instance, when a new client calls and inquires about your services, the more that you have your language prepared ahead of time, the less you have to think things up on the spot. A lot of people in holistic health care are very intuitive and they often respond emotionally, which can sometimes reduce how articulate they are in the moment. It really helps for them to know exactly what they're going to say when they want to invite someone to book an appointment with them. It's important to have those words down so that they don't even have to think and part of that needs to be how the client will benefit from the session with them.

We have to know what the issue is. We can't create scripts until we know where the boundary gets crossed.

Molly: This is a great topic because I think for many people who want to bring their business to a higher level, they don't even realize that this is part of what is holding them back: that they are letting people step on their boundaries, giving away too much, not asserting themselves. They may be feeling really tired and not realizing why they're feeling so ragged and depleted.

Roberta: Yes, they get depleted when they let people cross their boundaries. Here's a situation that happened to me. I had a client who had recently hired me, and she was already committed to a free three-day seminar on business expansion. This one was geared toward healers like herself. I got an email from her at 7:00 p.m. on the Saturday night of the program, saying she's about to sign up for this program and she must make a decision by 11:00 a.m. the following day. Should she do it? Her email implied that she wanted to talk with me on Sunday before 11 a.m. And mind you, this is Saturday night.

Molly: Is this an expensive program?

Roberta: Oh yeah. They don't give away a three-day seminar unless they're going to be selling something pretty costly at the end of it. I guess it was in the $6,000-$8,000 range for a ten-month program. So I read her email about 8 or 9 o'clock on Saturday night and I had to sit with that and decide what my boundary was. I had to decide how I was going to respond or even if I was going to respond. It was email, not a phone call. And I'm just like my clients. I care about helping people and yet, these were not my work hours. This was not a paid session. This was someone asking me a business question through email on a Saturday night.

Now, if an established client has something happen to them on a Saturday or Sunday and they contact me, I'm there for them. This doesn't happen a lot. This woman was a new client. So I wrote her back and told her that Sundays were my day off but I gave her a list of questions for her to consider in making her decision.

I suggested she write down why she was drawn to the program, and to list the problems in her business that she wanted to solve, how the program would address those issues, and what red flags came up for her about the program. I wanted her to think it through. She may come up with her own answer and not need me. The next morning she sent me an email telling me what she was thinking of doing. I wrote her back and told her I was about to go exercise but if she wanted to talk I would be home after 10:00. You see, I had to think about my own boundary. I could have just not responded, because it was an email I received on a day I don't work, so I could have chosen to ignore it until Monday.

I know business people who don't respond to business emails from Friday night until Monday morning. I know that is a good idea, but one I have not implemented. When you have a business that involves personal contact with people you are always facing this boundary issue. In this situation I thought it through, and in the end I decided to respond to her. The message here is to develop your ability to think though your choices so you remember to take your needs into consideration.

Molly: And it didn't feel like it was violating your boundary?

Roberta: No, I felt okay with it. But next time I might decide to do something different. It is important to take the time to think the situation through. Each time there is a challenging situation, it gives you the opportunity to clarify your boundaries. In time, you will find you are no longer overextending yourself.

Molly: That's the same type of thing bodyworkers might experience—a little different because it requires physically getting together, but it's the same thing in that it's about someone needing you during your time off. There may be a situation where a good client has an accident or something where they really need you, and you make an exception and help them.

Roberta: We do step up for a good client.

Becoming a more successful business owner is a matter of identifying what your issues are and finding solutions. It might be something external—you know you need a better location because the one you're in is too noisy. Or it is important that you get out into the world and attend events. But often it's work we need to do with ourselves, our inner work. For instance, I wasn't comfortable doing public speaking. I would work on things at home and I was good at identifying things, but I was uncomfortable speaking in front of a group. So I did some serious soul searching and figured out why I was afraid to speak about what I felt and believed. I think my view of business is distinct and important, yet I was afraid to speak about it.

I realized it was a self-esteem issue—somewhere in my life I was convinced that what I had to say wasn't important. I knew that if I were going to be comfortable writing and speaking, I would need to heal that limiting belief. So I committed to baby steps. I found somebody who helped me improve my writing and I started writing e-newsletters every two weeks. This was important for consistency. And as I received feedback from people that this was valuable to them, I started to trust that I had something worthwhile to say. Then I wrote a longer piece, which I turned into a free eBook that chronicles my challenges with expressing myself honestly. It is titled, *Know Your Value: How Owning Your Worth Impacts Your Income*. Your readers are welcome to contact me through my website and I will send them a copy. Over this past year, I've been doing public speaking. Now I'm not afraid to speak and I'm working on the skill building of being a good public speaker.

Molly: The emotional issues are so critical. A lot of healers worry about setting their rates. There are always people in the service industry offering low rates. Even though they may not be high quality, they are still part of the competition. I think this is true of all services. So it takes truly valuing yourself to charge enough.

Roberta: I agree completely. There are two different business models. One is low cost and volume, and the other is high cost and customized. It is important to know which model your business is. In massage, the chains are the high volume and low cost model. And then there are those highly skilled practitioners who do very unique, specific work. A bodyworker might look at the low cost chains and have fear about competing, even if what they offer is much higher quality. So their inner work is to increase their self-confidence so they charge what they're worth. Their outer work is to learn enough about marketing to effectively communicate their value to their client base.

We can go back to the question that set me on my quest: Two massage practitioners in the same community. One is doing extremely well and the other one is struggling. Why? It isn't the economy. It isn't the community. It has to be something within themselves and the way they are approaching each of their businesses. For the one that is struggling to change their situation, they would need to identify what the problem is. If it has to do with the way their office looks, then no amount of marketing is going to make a difference.

Molly: Is that what you do? Look at peoples' offices and recommend when they need to make changes?

Roberta: I don't tell people what to do. I help them discover it for themselves. This is the difference between coaching and consulting.

Molly: Oh! That's an interesting distinction. What is the difference between the two?

Roberta: I think of consultants as bringing in expertise. They say, here's how to handle this marketing. Or, here's a framework to use for your pricing structure. They give expertise. A coach is somebody who helps people come to their own answers.

Molly: Almost like a business therapist.

Roberta: Exactly. That is a great analogy. I actually do both consulting and coaching. There are some things, like a bookkeeping system, where I advise them on the best way to do it. But there are other things that people need to figure out on their own because there is no right answer. The most important part of my work is coaching my clients to develop their skills and confidence at assessing a situation so they can figure out the best solution. By the way, the skill of business problem solving is one that all successful business owners are very good at.

There are a million ways to promote yourself, and you just have to test them and figure out what works. By that, I mean both what's effective and what you enjoy doing. It's very individual. For instance, the woman I go to for haircuts sends me a thank you note and a coupon for half-off every time I send her a new referral. That has me actually thinking about referring more people to her. I would refer to her anyway, but this gives me a bit more incentive.

Business is a creative process. It is not uncommon for clients that begin work with me to say they hate marketing or business, or both, and then at some point during our work together they begin to enjoy the process.

Molly: Yes, I agree that it's incredibly creative. It's important to put yourself in the customer's shoes and ask yourself, what would appeal to me?

Roberta: That's exactly right. There's nothing wrong with business. There's a mindset in our culture about business not being okay.

Molly: I think that's because there's so much gimmicky stuff that goes on that it turns us off and we don't want to be associated with it.

If you're really honest and put what you have to offer out there in a way that is well expressed, people are going to get that—especially with something like bodywork. People are attracted to personalities. It's not just the way someone's thumb presses into a shoulder muscle, but it's the entire experience of spending an hour with someone whose personality and way of being you like. You walk out of there feeling great because you just got to spend an hour with someone really incredible.

Roberta: That reminds me of the woman I have gone to for massage who is really wonderful. I used to be on a very regular schedule with her. But lately, the way my schedule has been means I have to book at the last minute. And she's not able to accommodate that. So the last time I got a massage, I booked it with someone who is easier to get in to see. The other therapist has a really full life, and our schedules don't sync. I had to contact her by email and try to find a time when I could come in, and it was too complicated, going back and forth looking for a time that worked for both of us. Whereas the new massage therapist whom I met at a networking event had regular set hours so it was much easier to get an appointment with her.

Molly: Yes, people need to take a look at how they're sabotaging themselves, like the massage therapist you were going to whom you really loved but was hard to schedule.

Roberta: Yes. She's a great bodyworker. However, in all honesty, now that we are talking about it, maybe her lack of availability is connected to her honoring her boundaries.

Molly: This has been very valuable. Part of what I want to demonstrate to massage therapists who are getting their businesses started is that there's a lot more to having a business than a marketing strategy. People will think all they need to do is find a way to fill up their appointment book, but there's a lot more to business than that.

Roberta: It's like what we talked about earlier. You can have two people in the same town, both skilled, and one is busy and the other isn't. It's is easy to say the economy is bad or no one in massage makes a good living, but it is not true. Having a business is a huge personal growth experience. You learn a great deal about yourself through this process. You aren't just growing a business. You're growing as a person.

If you are sincere about your goal of a successful business, I suggest you invest time and money in learning to be "in business." You certainty would if you wanted to learn to play the piano. It doesn't need to be hugely time consuming or expensive—there are hundreds of free webinars, libraries full of books, and modestly priced programs everywhere. It's important to take yourself as a business owner seriously. You can start wherever you are and learn one thing at a time. It's also valuable to find enjoyment in the process.

Molly: That's beautifully put, Roberta. Thank you very much.

A note from Molly: I found it quite enlightening to talk to Roberta because a lot of what she does in her coaching practice is work with the emotional blocks that are holding people back. Setting prices and sticking to boundaries are both critical business issues that have to do with self-esteem and self-confidence. This can be at the core of whether someone is doing well or getting burned out.

A lot of the time, we are not able to recognize what is keeping us from succeeding. But a few sessions with a coach can show us where we are stuck. This can help us discover what we need to do to change our way of thinking and feeling so we can take care of ourselves at the same time we are taking care of our clients.

For more information:

www.robertaryan.com

Chapter 16: Guided Visualization - a Powerful Tool

You know that feeling of blissful confidence you have when you're "in the zone?" You're in the right place at the right time and you excel at whatever skill is called for in that moment. Whether you're giving a massage, cooking a meal, or showing a friend how to do something you're good at, there are times when you can bask in the pleasure of your own self-confidence. People are impressed with you, and you feel on top of the world. Everything falls into place. This is what success feels like.

When you feel successful and you are in the zone, the flow is effortless. You can take action and know that the outcome will be good. In fact, these are the times when it's easy to stretch yourself and take a risk.

I learned how to get into this frame of mind by listening to guided visualization recordings that were designed to uplift one's spirits and inspire confidence.

I did this a lot in the early days of my massage business when I needed the reassurance to keep going and try new things. Our thoughts have a profound effect on the way we feel. And the way we feel has a huge impact—not only in our actions, but in the way our actions are received by others. Listening to recordings helped put me into a good mental place about my practice and my life. I was able to have wonderful experiences with clients via that happy and energetic state of mind. I also attracted great opportunities that enabled me to connect with more people and share my work.

It's amazing how powerful our thoughts are. They affect our health, our personality, our self-image and the ability to move forward with our ideas. With a background in psychology, I was well aware how critical our thoughts were for good mental health.

It was this understanding that inspired me to study hypnosis and become certified as a hypnotherapist. At one point at about ten years into my practice, I realized that although my clients were getting physical relaxation from me, they still had mental loops that kept them tense. They would come to see me after work and I could tell their minds were churning. From the things they talked about, it was clear that they could not completely unwind because they were still mentally wrapped up in problems they were trying to solve.

I decided if I was really going to help them, I had to be able to guide them into relaxing their minds as well as their bodies. I contacted a colleague I knew from college studies in psychology, who had pursued a career in hypnosis and had created a school with a certification program. Randal Churchill's Hypnotherapy Training Institute is now one of the most renowned schools of hypnotherapy in the country.

I plunged head first into the hypnotherapy course. I was able to see immediately what a difference it made to focus my mind in a certain way. We don't realize it, but we are subtly being hypnotized all the time. Advertisers use these techniques to convince us that the products they are selling will make us happier, look better, feel better, etc. And through the power of repetitive suggestion, they are correct. People become convinced.

I used my hypnosis skills in the massage office to help my clients let go. I offered sessions where I taught them to slow down their minds and release the thoughts that were making them tense. Sometimes we can get caught up in a spiral, where the same thoughts keep circling around, not really getting us anywhere. This can continue to keep us obsessed about something over which, at the moment, we have no control.

When someone comes in for a massage, it is time to leave the stress behind. Whatever difficulties that person is dealing with, whether it's something at work or a personal relationship or something else, they aren't going to solve that problem while they are on your massage table. They are there for a break. But it can be hard for a person to let go of that mental loop.

I used very simple guided visualization techniques. Some clients would choose to get a double session, where they would spend the first hour letting go mentally through guided visualization followed by an hour of massage. It's a very powerful combination. Many of my clients loved it.

People also became interested in doing hypnosis for behavioral changes and to overcome fears and addictions to things like tobacco, so I offered hypnosis sessions separately, in addition to massage. I also took more classes, as different situations presented themselves and there was more I wanted to learn.

This is often how you end up specializing in additional modalities. You experience something that you personally find powerful, something that affects your own health so profoundly you'll be inspired to incorporate it into your practice so your clients can benefit from it as well.

I started making guided visualization recordings for my clients so they had something they could take home with them and listen to over and over. Each time they listened to the recording, it reinforced the session we had. I also made these recordings for myself when there was something I needed to change.

When I wrote this book, I decided to make a success recording for my readers so you could lie down, close your eyes and visualize your ideal practice. It's called "Successful Strokes" and it's a 20-minute guided journey that will help put you in the right frame of mind to create the kind of business you really want. The recording is designed to give you confidence and the awareness that you have everything you need to fill your practice and create the kind of lifestyle you are visualizing. The more you listen to it, the more these feelings become part of you.

This is a perfect way to spend an unscheduled hour. You can take a break, stretch out on the massage table, listen to the recording, and get a clear picture of the practice you want to create. You will then find it easy to take the necessary steps to make that happen.

 After this chapter, I have a full list of the recordings I have made, which you can purchase online.

This is an exciting and creative adventure. Follow your heart. Trust your gut. You have my blessing!

Molly Kurland

GUIDED VISUALIZATION RECORDINGS

The following recordings are available on iTunes, Google Play Music, or Amazon Digital Music. You can find these recordings at www.successfulstrokes.com/recordings.

Successful Strokes: Launching Your Massage Business, narrated by Molly Kurland

Description: This is a recording to help you become successful from the inside out. By letting the words guide you and imagining the details of your profitable practice you will develop the confidence of a successful massage therapist. You will attract a devoted clientele who are attracted to your positive energy. 20 minutes.

Sink Into Sleep, narrated by Molly Kurland (under the Travel Whisperers label)

Description: Let these words lull you to sleep. Whatever you have planned for tomorrow, it doesn't matter right now, because all you need to focus on is the softness of the pillow, the caress of the warm, cozy sheets and letting yourself sink deeply into a delicious night of uninterrupted sound sleep. 20 minutes.

The Travel Series

Each recording is carefully worded to help you adjust to the various aspects of traveling. Every album contains three tracks: a male voice, a female voice and a track with both voices.

Sleeping on a Plane narrated by Molly Kurland and Bill Kennedy (under the Travel Whisperers label)

Description: Retreat into your own world, oblivious to any distractions so that you can easily fall sleep in flight and arrive relaxed and alert.

Sleeping Away from Home narrated by Molly Kurland and Bill Kennedy (under the Travel Whisperers label)

Description: This is a natural sleep aid that will help you teach your body and mind to relax, helping you feel at home and at peace wherever you are.

Time Zone Shift narrated by Molly Kurland and Bill Kennedy (under the Travel Whisperers label)

Description: This is a remedy for jet lag. By imagining yourself in the new time zone you automatically make internal shifts that affect your circadian rhythm giving signals to your body of when to eat and sleep so you can arrive refreshed.

ADDITIONAL RESOURCES

I hope this book has given you great ideas for creating and growing your bodywork practice. Here are other things that I offer.

Coaching: If you would like some personal attention, I offer coaching, either by phone or via Skype. This is an opportunity to have support as you map out a plan to get your business under way. It can make a big difference to have someone who can answer your questions, as well someone to be accountable to so that you are certain follow through on the steps you have laid out. If you want help and specific guidance, please contact me through my website.

www.successfulstrokes.com

Blog: This is where I write about many things that I find restorative for one's personal growth, including a series of posts on self-care. You can find it here:

fillmyspirit.wordpress.com

Visit my Facebook Page. I share inspirations, articles related to the field of bodywork and a variety of things to support you.

facebook.com/successfulstrokesmassagebook

ACKNOWLEDGEMENTS

Putting this book together was a long and complicated process. I learned so much and am so grateful to have a community of writers and friends who were able to advise and help me get it done.

Thanks to Carol Venolia, friend, author, and editor par excellence who edited the first version of this book for me. She encouraged me to publish and get the book from my hard drive, where I thought it would sit forever, and out into the world.

I am extremely grateful to my critique group buddies, Inga Aksamit and Norma Smith Davis, who gave me such great feedback and editing as I rewrote each chapter and added more content to the book. Having our regular meetings gave me deadlines that made sure I got the work done.

Crissi Langwell helped me in many ways. She did the final touches that made the book look good and read well. And she made me a beautiful blog so I could write posts about things that matter to me.

George Buce, brilliant tech wizard, designed me a beautiful website, more artistic than I could have imagined.

Kim Munkres, my dear friend, read sections and gave me her honest opinions, as well as talking me off the ledge when needed.

Thanks to Ed Lark, Roberta Ryan, and Ona Goodrich for agreeing to be interviewed so I could show some more perspectives to my readers.

And I am appreciative more than I can possibly say to the many massage therapists that have been part of my life over the years. We traded massage. We traded stories. We supported each other through the ups and downs of self-employment and we made life more fun for each other. I particularly appreciate my early readers: Sarah Pedlow, Wendy Levy, Cynthia Mealy, Roberta Gabriel, Sherry Aquilino, Stephanie Stone, Kanti Pike, Julie Callahan, and Nina Morre. You helped me make my dream real.

And thanks to my creative genius husband, Miles Kurland, for making me a beautiful professional book cover.

You are my community and family. We don't do this alone.

Molly has worked in the field of massage for over twenty years. She started with a solo private practice developing success strategies, which inspired the content of this book. She eventually expanded the business into a day spa that included aesthetics and a gift shop. She uses her years of business experience, as well as her background in psychology, to show that having a successful practice involves a lot more than marketing. There are a great many subtleties that go into having a business that is both appealing to the public and deeply satisfying for the therapist.

Molly became a hypnotherapist in order to help her clients unwind mentally as well as physically. She incorporates hypnosis into her practice, sometimes doing separate sessions of hypnosis and sometimes doing hypnosis first to relax the mind and then following it with massage to relax the body. She also makes guided visualization recordings.

To learn more visit: www.successfulstrokes.com.

www.ingramcontent.com/pod-product-compliance
Lightning Source LLC
Chambersburg PA
CBHW072100020426
42334CB00017B/1575